New Boots and
Pantisocracies

New Boots and Pantisocracies

edited by W.N. Herbert
and Andy Jackson

Smokestack Books
1 Lake Terrace, Grewelthorpe, Ripon HG4 3BU
e-mail: info@smokestack-books.co.uk
www.smokestack-books.co.uk

ISBN 978-0-9934547-5-2

Published in cooperation with Gairfish

Smokestack Books is
represented by Inpress Ltd

Contents

MINISTRY OF PEACE

MINISTRY OF PLENTY

MINISTRY OF TRUTH

Editor's Introduction

Over the three key political events of the last three years – the Scottish referendum, the General Election of 2015, and the recent EU referendum – the idea of the UK as a single country (still conflated here and elsewhere with 'England') has been replaced by a plurality of identities, some long known to its other countries, regions, and religions, others formulating themselves as time passes.

For these reasons, then, back in 2015, we thought it might be an interesting experiment to chart the responses of those unacknowledged legislators, the poets, over the first 100 days of the new government. We ended up publishing a poem a day for 138 days, each one responding to some aspect of the new unrealpolitik. We then set to editing a book of 100 poems in order to, as we thought then, conclude the project.

In fact, the EU Referendum results showed that the slow slew in British political identity toward disillusionment and division had reached a breaking point that made even more evident the contrasts already indicated by the Scottish referendum and the General Election.

Post-Brexit – or, rather, at the time of writing, in the midst of the Phony Brexit or protracted limbo before the activation of Article 50 – the new uncertainties have almost ripped the Labour Party apart, while a generation of Tories have been sluiced away, howling, into the ignominious dark, and a new generation (plus a few revenants) slotted neatly and with gleaming tooth into their vacated stalls.

It is therefore likely that, as with the knights supposedly slumbering beneath numerous mountains – some made of granite, others perhaps of butter – ready to rise in their tribe's or nation's or language's hour of need, we'll be going round with a pointy stick from time to time, stirring up the poets like metrical myrmidons or bardic bureaucrats, and urging them to issue yet another scroll-ful of unratified rulings.

Whether this means a subsequent volume of New Boots and Pantisocracies may become, as the victory of the proletariat was long regarded, inevitable, we have at the moment no way of knowing. Stick with our blog (https://newbootsandpantisocracies.wordpress.com) while we negotiate whatever the hell happens next.

*

By way of introduction to our unusual title, we should say it is, properly, a portmanteau term. It combines the title of Ian Dury's marvellous debut album of 1977 with the name given in 1794 by the young Romantic poets, Samuel Coleridge and Robert Southey, to their scheme to set up what we would still like to think of as a socialist society in America, a failed utopian project reimagined by Paul Muldoon in his 1990 poem, 'Madoc: A Mystery', as actually happening:

> 'Twelve months ago they embarked, de dum, Te Deum,
> on a merchantman out of Rotterdam
>
> and were seen off from the Bristol quay
> by a bemused citizenry
>
> including Hucks and Cottle, their fellow-
> Pantisocratics, who now dismissed the plan as folly.'

As with Bremainers today, or those Scots left bankrupt by the 1690s folly of the Darien Expedition, or the emancipatory scheme put into action by the Dundonian freethinker and abolitionist Frances Wright as the Nashoba Community on the banks of the Wolf River, Tennessee, in 1825, the continuing energy of Pantisocracy is all in the might-have-beens, the imaginative resonance of the alternative history if not an alternative to history. So far.

As those of you with an interest in popular music will know, Dury's *New Boots and Panties* is now regarded as a classic of a different sort of alternative: punk, the rejection of an industry that, it was argued, had betrayed its origins in the rebellion and artistic autonomy of rock and roll. The pomp of prog and the profit-worshipping of major record labels were considered to have alienated a youth audience from music itself, substituting a range of ersatz commodities, and marketing these as integral parts of their compromised identity.

Ian Dury, by contrast, deployed punk's defining trope of seizing not just the means of production, but the materials, in the simultaneous acts of creating music and creating the self of the musician. By this means the listener becomes the maker, and the passive becomes active, often politically as much as artistically. He reappropriated a wealth of styles, and fused funk, rock'n'roll, and music hall styles with flashes of disco and pub rock, to produce a transgressive, typically English, radically working class sound.

Those of us who encountered it in our teens knew immediately it was something we shouldn't play when our parents were listening, with its tales of early-morning sexual encounters, shady dealings, and *that* opening line to 'Plaistow Patricia'.

The compelling album cover art featured Dury standing outside Axford's underwear and lingerie shop at 306 Vauxhall Bridge Road, Westminster back in '77. This was an important link to the album title, which referred to the only items of clothing which Dury thought should always be bought new rather than second-hand.

A slice of the artwork features as our own cover art on the blog, and a brilliant, scabrous variation on it by the poet and artist Tim Turnbull graces the cover of this book.

In true Dury style, then, the punning title of this poetry project arose from a conversation on Facebook with Donut Press's editor, Andy Ching, in the week after the election. The phrase just arrived, and the way it bounced Dury's ripe knowingness off Southey and Coleridge's early idealism suddenly seemed to make sense of our current bewilderment. It combined cynicism with a sense that, contra Postmodern ennui, we nonetheless had to act. It was, we realised, one of those rare spontaneous puns you look again at and think, 'What can I do with that?'

But here it was evident that it would be more of a case of what other poets could do with it. Key to that was a simpatico co-editor who would have lots of their own ideas, and lots of energy if not necessarily time (who, after all, is allowed to have time?), so, having worked with him on *Whaleback City*, and having seen what he did with *Double Bill* and other anthologies for Red Squirrel, Andy Jackson was the obvious choice.

Many other writers have taken the project to heart not just as contributors and distributors – sharers and retweeters – but also volunteering suggestions and help: Harry Giles and Rachael Boast have been particularly generous in this regard. Andy Croft was keen to publish as soon as we asked. Thanks to them all.

We liked the idea of it being founded in a snap of verbal energy as much as a moment of political righteousness, and the results have borne that out, amounting to a poetic more than a polemic. There's plenty of anger and bewilderment, but these are lines of poetry rather than unwavering expressions of a party line, and their energy comes from a collision of the verbal with the visceral, a recharging of language even as it is being emptied by our political masters and their envious opposites.

We anticipated the initial stages might be caught up in a necessary hangover of shock, anxiety, and disappointment, but then were delighted by how that developed into a nuanced vision of the various social reconfigurations going on across not just these islands, but throughout Europe and beyond. From the start we wanted a wide range of writing, by which we meant the throwaway as well as the weighty, the traditional as well as the radical, the deadly serious as well as the absurd and the satirical. By the time of the first Tory budget, we knew that, unlike George Osborne, we had something to share that was genuinely imaginative.

A real concern was the usual rush of many white males to respond, countered by a slower but increasingly steady stream of material from women poets and poets of colour of both genders. Some people do just respond more spontaneously, while others prefer to consider things at length, but it is sobering to note that this still tends to follow predictable lines.

(The strong early response from Scottish writers might have been because we have been considering things since before the Referendum if not since the Reformation.)

Here the decision to run for 100 days gradually bore fruit, as did the editorial habit of approaching people as and when throughout, rather than keeping to an inflexible 'must have' checklist. In fact, quite a few of the usual 'must haves' didn't seem to be on any of our scribbled and frequently updated lists. No doubt some of them were unfortunate omissions, but it did seem like part of the 'new boots' rubric had to be about hearing new voices.

Open submissions did not, for once in the poetry world, flood in, despite our decision to give a fifth of the project over to them, but thankfully the work we received fulfilled that original remit of delivering surprising and exciting new angles.

*

A slightly different but no less important concern here might be the question of bias. This is, unashamedly, a left-leaning, if not left-shoulder to the wheel, if not left-falls down, but gets back up again, kind of book. Although the constraints of editing a daily blog meant we did not canvas their opinions explicitly, the agendas of many of its contributors – conflicted as they might be on fundamental aspects of Labour policy and the more (and often less) interesting postures of its representatives – do not on the whole appear very sympathetic to the practices of neoliberalism, whether they be disaster capitalism, media manipulation, eco-asset stripping, or good old racist demagoguery.

This might feel like solidarity, but as always, runs the risk of amounting to little more than confirmation bias. Surely it is an issue that no writers appearing to hold even a slightly right of centre position were comfortable enough to consider submitting? Or does the issue go rather to the types of actions of the imagination, or attitudes toward thought and experience, that produce poems? After all, there are plenty of conservative thinkers happy enough to beard the Lefties in the prose discourses of the media and the public meeting. Is this a failure of poetry, or of politics?

What we have here, after all, goes beyond a simplistic left/right axis. This is politics reimagined as satire, as elegy, as fantasmagoria if not vision, and as eulogy. Each of these have been as possible, historically, for the right as the left. We have an activist, even a propagandist, poetics in MacDiarmid's useful definition ('...any utterance that is not pure / Propaganda is impure propaganda for sure!') – again, equally possible for both parties. The touchy, curmudgeonly, nit-picky poet is all too possible to the point of approaching the clichéd norm. So why is there, apparently, no kontemporary Kiplingesque kipperer of any kwality?

The answer may lie in a combination of two factors: what do we think validates a form of words as 'poetic'; and what, for most of us, constitutes 'significant' discourse?

The first plays out an old antagonism between the rhetorical and the lyrical, in which Romantic ideas of emotional authenticity still have the casting vote. Yeats's adage about the argument with others being, dismissively, rhetoric, would make little sense to Cicero, for whom the well-formed argument was a moral necessity, and therefore the main point of focus, not who made it to whom. As he argues in *Academica*:

> '...the sole object of our discussions is by arguing both sides to draw out and give shape to some result that may be either true or the nearest possible approximation of the truth.'

As Michael Mendelson points out in his essay 'Everything Must Be Argued', from which I take the previous quote, this indicates 'a dramatist orientation' toward the world, where the ability to understand the other is the paramount means by which we arrive, not at a persuasive version of our opinion, but at an overview of whatever that is which is the case. In short: Shakespeare, not Yeats.

Coleridge, when discussing Shakespeare's 'Venus and Adonis' in the *Biographia Literaria*, seems to map out something of this rhetorically if not necessarily politically responsible poetic:

> 'I think, I should have conjectured from these poems, that even then the great instinct, which impelled the poet to the drama, was secretly working in him, prompting him... to provide a substitute for that visual language, that constant intervention

and running comment by tone, look and gesture, which in his dramatic works he was entitled to expect from the players... The reader is forced into too much action to sympathize with the merely passive of our nature.'

By contrast, the lyric is intimate in focus as well as subject, being the song to another overheard by the many, rather than the dialogue, or the address to a multitude. But if its authenticity can only be guaranteed by the subjective authority of strong feelings, then a political poetry is reduced to who feels the deepest, loudest, or longest. And what further validation is there for that, except from outside the poem, in the realm of identity politics: the virtuous stamp of the righter-on-than-thou brigade, or the literal stamp of the right?

The problem here is assessment therefore proceeds by faith, as acts of sympathy or sentiment rather than sensibility or criticism. And here is where the second issue, of the significance of any given discourse, comes into play.

Most people mistake most poetry for the lyrical, whereas, as Coleridge implies, throughout the best poetry, working as it were undercover in some cases, all nine muses continue to operate and cooperate. For political poetry, then, the governing muses are more Clio and Calliope, the muses of history and epic, than Euterpe or Erato.

But if our perception of poetry is that it is typically Euterpical, or erratically Eratic – subjective, sentimental, and generally under represented on the political stage, as well as in the media which reports on that stage – then why should we turn to it to engage with any matter in the public arena? That which we regard as, strictly, for the nearest and dearest, cannot by this definition reach very far.

Perhaps, then, the more self-important among us will not utilise a form they regard, or can see is regarded, as unimportant, unless their self-importance outweighs their desire to influence, rather than to affect, others.

Now, this is not to say there aren't at least as many self-important people on the left as on the right. What folly that would be. Rather it is to suggest that for the right, politics may seem more a matter of pragmatics, while for the left it could appear more a matter of principle. In that case, the misunderstood medium of poetry, is, respectively, less and more likely to be their first port of call.

To refer back to the examples of Dury, Southey and Coleridge, if you don't think of art as a way of creating identity and of empowerment, perhaps that is because your identity has been satisfactorily shaped for you, and you have a secure enough power base to build from without stooping to concur.

*

Throughout the 138 days we kept asking ourselves 'Do we have a book?' Because there was no particular pressure for New Boots to become one – the blog format suited the ephemerality of the project in the literal sense of living for the day, not only seizing it, but being sufficient unto it, dwelling in the moment of the line as much as the headline, and we hoped we were particularly alive to the resonance of that phrase used at the beginning of this introduction: 'at the time of writing'.

We further hoped, if nothing else, that we were assembling a substantial, diverse, and exciting selection of the best of contemporary poetry, but we kept anticipating that point when the work became something more: not just a response to the moment, but a record of and memorial to it, something both feisty and geisty in relation to der Zeit. What we were after was a totality that might equate to a slightly more optimistic collective noun than the media stereotype – neither a paranoia of poets, nora pretension, but that lost ideal (crossed with just the slightest hint of smut), a pantisocracy. That, we thought, might make a book worth reading.

Whether we achieved it or not is up to you, the reader, to decide. Please feel free to use our social media platforms on Wordpress, Facebook, and Twitter to debate the point.

Finally, a word about the organization of this book, which alludes of course to the work of that great polemicist, George Orwell. By dividing the work according to the four ministries of Airstrip One in *Nineteen Eighty-four*, we are not just having a dig at the attitudes of the political class, which the EU Referendum revealed in their full duplicity, partisanship, myopia, and hubristic disarray, but also indicating that the opinions expressed in these pages are not without their own ideologies, admitting we all may be as guilty of partiality as any journalist who pretends they're not really following their newspaper's owner's agenda.

Where we place our faith, after all, is in the rhetorical, formal, musical, and symbolic power of the poem, not just to move or to persuade, but to present to us how it is to be within an historical moment, constantly struggling, not to transcend it but to confront it, with all our senses, our conscience and our intellect alive to its beauty, its terror, and its transience.

That seems to us to be where, on a daily basis, poetry and politics meet, and where each may transform the other. We like to think it is a point on which, at a certain point in their respective careers, Ian Dury, Robert Southey, and Samuel Taylor Coleridge, might all have concurred.

W.N. Herbert

Ministry
of Love

At The Standard

I cried all morning, said Francesca.
It's bad, I said. *It's bad*, came her echo.
Wrong world. *A pint of Becks please*,
this to the barmaid, *and a cure for hay feve*r.
Get pregnant, she says. *It works*. Wrong
crawls all over the menu here. Spoilt
when our wallet spills. Once, we had
powsowdie, then microwaved macaroni.
Now our buns are glazed, omega seeds
are scattered. *Make the profiteroles large
to share*. That polecat rubs his mitts
in number ten. There is summer slaw,
kale pesto. Everything comes smothered.
Skin-on. Quinoa rules this establishment.
Standard. Sourdough, stout-cured, heritage.
I picture Cameron, ginger ale ketchup
infecting the razoredgant where his chin
might have developed. *I've heard of it*,
is the most he can offer on disbelief.
Deep in the caliphate, knives are whetted.
America boils on borrowed gas. Baby gem
sounds tasty, but I long back sussed
that life is largely lies swanked up
and fed to you cold. Dearie me, fuck this.

Roddy Lumsden

New Boots and Panties

We stayed in the pub, election night.
There were a few of us: the guv'nor,
the usual lads, some of the ever-popular
drunk sorts and the feisty Welsh barmaid.
By the time we clocked red London was sinking
we were tossing back the drinks,
less for the fun of it and more to lose the taste.
The jukebox took a beatin' too –
reggae and punk. Songs from our yoof.
Babylon's Burning, I remember that all right.
Beasley Street was my choice.
We were up at the bar reciting along:
'Keith Joseph smiles and a baby dies...'
The Welsh girl asked who he was.
In honesty, the lilt of her voice deserved
a better answer. 'He just moved in,' I told her,
'you'll be hearing a lot about him.'
Come the weekend she caught me by the elbow,
'I looked that Keith Joseph up,' she said.
'He seems like a proper cunt.'

Tim Wells

Zimbardoland

So successful
were the trials that
we've recommended
the method be
rolled out nationwide
with immediate effect
adding one refinement
that's a stroke
of HR wizardry
whereby the subjects
in the interests
of efficiency
have been persuaded
to press their own buttons.

Go on. Press it.
You know you want to.

Tim Turnbull

from a better tale to tell
a found poem derived from public
submissions to the Smith Commission

good morning Lord Smith

hello

if we are more involved
more able to be involved
then we will become

more forgiving

more proactive

more grown-up

please

we must have our own powers
there are no advantages
for us here

values are to do with
the moral life

experienced in companionship
with other people

they are not derived
from a nationalist or unionist
lexicon

the Union flag to be flown
on all public buildings
where the Satire is flown
go back to Scotland the Brave
at sporting matches

p.s. OK the last one won't happen
but Flower of Scotland is dire

Federalism
raises the problem
of what to do
in England

there seems little appetite
to recreate

>   *Wessex*
>   *Mercia*
>   *Northumbria*

as states of the union
a new English parliament
is a necessity
of any settlement
whether the English
want it or not

Scotland is
one of the most
beautiful countries
on earth

I am constantly in awe
of our landscape of fields
merging into the river Forth

the threat

and I truly believe it is a threat
of fracking looms

please note

my complete objection
to fracking

I urge you to say
NO to fracking in Scotland

Scottish rocks
are naturally fracked
due to how ancient they are

they have moved around a lot
and are cracked and fractured
already

Scottish water
should not be used to supply
even English fracking

pleasepleaseplease
do not allow this

change is risk
we could get it wrong

we have nothing
to fear

I have no easy answers

that would be to put my-
self on a pedestal

but it is not just
my voice

please do not return
to your remote ways

thanks for listening
I hope to hear back from you

yours with still a bit of
hope left in my heart

composed by Alec Finlay

The Chase

Hell might have a Function Room like this,
Where gravy fights it out with Harpic:
A mock-Tudor Midland roadhouse,
Thirties-built to meet the passing trade
Long since diverted down the bypass,
It fell on hard times, then on harder ones
And kept on falling through false floors,
Down shafts of optimistic anaglypta,
Past the cheap and cheerful weddings,
Underbooked conventions, lingerie events
And charismatic preachers braving out
The years God turned his face away.

The old place stands in hawthorn scrub
Beside the nibbled Chase, its car-park
Dogged by doggers. It must long for arson.
What it gets are damaged veterans
And others of uncertain provenance,
Would-be *Werwolfs*, left behind
To serve the cause from bunkers dug
Beneath allotments their St George's flags
Announce are Ingerland no more.
There will be those who speak, who bring
Fraternal greetings from 'our Flemish friends'
And those who listen with a hope so long
Deferred it is immortal. What began
One pale late summer evening here
Will end when darkness brings instructions
To prepare for the eternal Soon,
The ur-time worshipped in the true
Theology where things are otherwise.
But in the meantime minutes must be taken,
Grist to the banal resentments,
Nudges, localized atrocities, as omens of
The greater cause, and let no one forget

That there are windows to be licked
And public discourse to be joined
Until, on average eighteen seconds in,
The call's cut off at Radio Chase ('It's where
The middle of the Midlands is') again.

These are the relatives you never see now
Since your parents' generation died.
You do remember, yes, the awkwardness –
A funeral tea held somewhere like the Chase,
That might have even been the Chase,
A flyblown nowhere, birches, ponds,
With HGVs parked up in laybys full of rubbish
And a sense that give or take this could be
Any time since 1931.
And someone's husband joining you outside
To smoke, assuming you'd agree
With his shy-smiling bigotry about
'Our friends from the subcontinent.'
You can't remember what you said. You can,
And it was nothing, while he stood his ground
There in the carpark, and if he sensed
That you were clenching with embarrassment
You couldn't tell. He'd made his point,
While you declared you'd better make a start
And he advised what roads you should avoid,
And never blinked, while here in hindsight
You're still blinking at the shame of it
When accident has brought you back
Down these unfashionable routes,
And then contrived the need to stop
And get a sandwich.
                              Sunday afternoon
In Albion's excluded middle.
The meeting is concluding on the far side
Of the corridor. The literature is all there
At the back beside the runes and ornamental
Daggers that make lovely gifts. To say it takes

All sorts may be a fallacy, but here they are
And here you are, again. The sandwich comes.
You watch them load their tat and nonsense
Back into the knacker's van. You are confused
By a persistent disbelief that this
Can be the case, this levee of Poujadists
Dawdling by their cars till those with homes
To go to go there, and those with holes
Hole up to count the days till their black sun
Rises on this honest plain of Midland
Ash and spoil and their inheritance is saved
From everyone, including you.
Too bored to laugh, too tired to cry, you think
These people do not matter. Then they do.

Sean O'Brien

Taverns Measureless to Man

After an evening at The Rummer Hotel
we leave by the side door into the back alley
glad in a way for the taste of the shake-up
having never sampled anything like it before.
Walking into the street, our pockets stuffed
with pamphlets on Pantisocracy, everything
looks different. What hasn't changed
are the facades of the buildings and the nails
outside the Corn Exchange. The women
are all over the place, legs and ankles
exposed to the strangely fresh air,
panties showing slightly beneath their skirts,
faces healthier than ever before, their hair
bizarre colours. Turning into Vine Street
we think of STC and the lyrical balladry
where Cottle's bookshop might have been.
The masts of the ships are nowhere to be seen.
What kind of trade arrangement is that, we jib,
TTIP, my arse, as we head for Castle Park
on the floating harbour. The bombed-out church
looks good at night, with its herb garden
well tended, fragrant with what we can preserve
of human hope in radical times. I give you
Compass Plant, Lavender, and Peace Flower,
rubbing it in as deeply as I can. Take my hand.
Your sweaty palm softens my skin
which, as usual, is burning with the sorrows
of our generation. Don't get political on me,
you say, we can do that later. Be my nature spirit,
my trade route and my produce;
be my Breakfast Martini, my Depth Bomb, my Rum Flip.

Rachael Boast

Shadow Cabinet

Appointed apparitions, although
your composition's pale and lacks
the resilience of past administrations
I like to think you'll break the silent
habit of the understudy, choosing,
when your duplicates step into the sun,
to turn left when they turn right
as solid opposition.
                          But since there is
five years to plot, the lost electorate
will wait as they have waited, deep
in nowhere dark, conceding their regrets
amongst the disappointed shades,
for the dreamed alternative to rise up
from the backbenches and eclipse the light.

John Challis

Probably, The Bell Curve

Probability dictates a world
where no one trips,
no one stumbles,
where no accident occurs
exists.

In some corner of this multiverse,
on some planet spinning
below a just right sun,
some language with no word for *luck*
exists.

A place where no stray cosmic ray
bounces a cell to cancer,
where the precarious bridge breaks
the second after landfall's made
exists.

Each child's fall from a tree's
cushioned by a mossy bank
or passing pal,
each swerving car on black ice
misses

the long and laughing bus stop queue.
Even the *Drano* bottle you swig's
been swapped for orange juice.
Fortune dances at the far end of the bell curve here.
Yes.

Somewhere out there, probably,
a world where the coin always falls
on the side you call,
where the safety net is never needed,
exists.

But it's not here.

A.F. Harrold

Building a Brighter, More Secure Future

Conservative Party election manifesto slogan, 2015

You must understand what we are building
is not the housing we promised. Not a
hospital, or school. It is a brighter
notion, an idea of Britain, where more
food banks will flourish, but for those secure
there is no cause for alarm. The future

is a place where the rich hand the future
to the poor, in which the great buildings
of Canary Wharf, climbing secure
above Tower Hamlets, offer up a
glut of wealth to the unfortunate, more
than you can imagine. This is a brighter

future, we promise, it is much brighter
than a concept like equality. A future
cannot be built on that. We all want more,
and some people are better at building
wealth, or else inheriting it, so a
tax for those who are beyond secure

is unfair: they made their money secure
through society, and being brighter –
or otherwise having been born to a
fortune – will make sure that in the future
sometime, this trickles down. As a building
stands firm, you have our word that more

will come to those without. Making more
is paramount to our concerns. To secure
this, in the meantime we have cuts building
steadily, to public services that the brighter,
more secure have no need for. In the future
you may need them, but the future is a

notion, distant and unknowable, it is a
distraction. What we are promising is more.
What we promise is a secure future
and this will be true, for some. More secure
as the great sun of the City shines brighter,
casts its shadow. Look what we are building.

This is our future. What we have is a
mandate to fulfil, building a Britain more
secure. And for us, it will be brighter.

Ben Wilkinson

In The Snug

Little man, you are my grinning birthright,
frog-faced in your better bookie's coat.
You lean against the ale-damp bar of England

and stroke the giggling landlady's chubby hand,
cooing words that stick in bigots' throats.
Little man, you are my chortling birthright –

an army of nothing waits on your command,
as you feed us one more slightly racist joke
and lean across the sticky bar of England

to pinch the fascist barmaid's arse. This land
is randy for the fear that you invoke.
Little man, you are my smirking birthright –

chief soother of our small, yet viscous band
that sneers at Johnny Foreigner, would gloat
to see him dashed against the rocks of England.

In the snug, your fog-horn voice demands
our rapt attention – true and piercing note
that holds us to you, little man. Our birthright
soaks into the blood-warm bar of England.

David Clarke

The Government

It wasn't me and it can't have been you
but I'm afraid to have to tell you that
somebody voted for the government.

The government don't know where they came from,
thousands of votes seemingly out of the blue,
but not from me and surely not from you.

We should have seen it coming, I suppose,
but what a dreadful day for politics
when somebody votes for the government.

Like the old joke, no matter how you vote
you always end up with the government
but I wouldn't vote for this lot. Would you?

We were so enthusiastic before.
We had our dreams, big plans for the future,
till someone voted for the government.

There can only be one explanation
but it doesn't give me pleasure to say
that if it wasn't me, it must be you
who bloody voted for the government.

Paul McGrane

Cleaning up

benches with no backs
and pigeon spikes for people

we'll have no roosting here
no rough sleep roosting here

no rough rest roost no
we'll have none of it

no beggars here
no empty tin can hand out

believe me we're well rid
of in the red

and when we rewrite riding hood
the wolf will win

no cosy welfare for a granny
idling in a bed

old and idling is no way to be
we're for the wolf's initiative

his bootstrap drive
and problem solving nous

and as for axes
let the woodsman fell the trees

we love a burning a burning
a burning

Jan Dean

The Torches and the Trees

after Vasko Popa

When the torches came
and people were smoked from pits,
fire took their homes.
And so they baffled up the streets
for those other people
pushing to get past.

Then the torches said
the trees must burn
to keep the people warm.
Thereupon the island was reborn
into a charcoal sketch
of empty hands.

When overnight the torches
transmuted into trees,
the people walked about
and tarried in their shelter.
Up up high in the branches,
the torches and their ending fire.

Helen Ivory

Brief

The point of pantisocracy
was all about democracy
equality, fraternity
and zero aristocracy.

In Glesga/Belfast/Leeds/Penzance
we didn't bank on folks in Hants
being anti-pantisocraphants.
Forget the sock. The outcome's pants.

*

PS: Aspheterism
When one is drinking herbal tea
and feeling thus bereft
one must remember, selflessly
that proper tea is theft.

Claudia Daventry

Revenge is a Dish

Revenge is not a dish.
Hot it's criminality. Cold it's a mental health issue.
Forgiveness is a meal in itself.

Robin Cairns

Brother

Some things are more important than family
Brother. I was chosen and you were not
Brother, does that mean there must be
an ocean between us Brother? Did our
mother suffer in the war for this Brother?
Was father not a good and clever man
Brother? Did they not teach us well
at the table Brother, was it unbidden
Brother, was I to be, Brother, always
at your heel Brother, am I Jacob, you
Esau Brother or Abel Brother or which
of us is Romulus and who is Liam
and who is Noel Brother? Don't tell
me the Party is changeful Brother. I believe
I've been badly lit Brother. O Brother
was it the blue sky or the Scottish bother
Brother or that the birds in the garden
have pins for eyes Brother? Can the people
be tired of Islington Brother, of justice
and equality Brother, are they so easily
bought Brother? I don't think it is
I didn't think enough Brother, perhaps
it was my goony face Brother or my
kitchens or unmasked secret lovers
Brother, the hen party selfies Brother
or the bacon sandwich that cast me out
Brother. Was it an angry God Brother,
was it that I was not you Brother, was it
stone Brother? Hold your clever tongue
for the sake of the movement Brother.
Be soundless as an owl Brother,
for it was for me, not you, to fall Brother.

Martin Figura

Enemy Within

Summer of 2015

They fall open-mouthed but silenced
through thunderstorms, sheet lightning,
fumes of meat, wet cement and drains,
falling through chewed grey litter
of lost forms, refusals, through futures
moth- and rust-corrupted by a cockroach parliament's
clicks and scuttles, jaws like gin traps
devouring us down to our marrow
for we too are falling, only slo-mo,
dreamless, as if in mourning
while *intelligence* accrues in rooms
with no address, passed innocently by trains:
we fall as if distant, electrical,
estranged from the blow, its bruise
but ordinary weather closes in,
we fall as rain drips through concrete
to mark a body in its sleeping-bag,
we fall as shame feeds its spores
on the last crusts, the butts of cigarettes,
cot sheets left out in the rain,
sanctions sanctioned.
We fall into nothingness
our cockroaches call *life*
which, like *money*, is never satisfied.

Pippa Little

Bear's Breeks: an irregular ode

'I want for my part
  Only the little white rose of Scotland'
Hugh MacDiarmid

The acanthus of rather a lot of Mediterranean countries is not for me.
I want for my part
Only the Bear's Breeks of Greece
Of which one might exclaim:
O Attic Shape! Hot pastoral!
What attitude this national flower displays!
It teases us out of constipation and shooteth forth
Very many large sad green smooth leaves
Upon the gound with a very thick
And juicy middle rib.

It has inspired Corinthian columns,
Is very good for tea
And is in the Bible.
In fonder moments
Think of it as cousin
To the thistle.

It is an excellent good plant
Under the dominion of the moon.
In clisters it mollifies the belly
And makes the passage slippery.
It unites shattered bones and strengthens
Joints that have been put well and truly out.
It is absolutely ace for the king's evil
That is broken and runneth.

In short, it restores radical moisture.

David Kinloch

All of Us Nervous

See me in me heels and ting
dem check say we hip and ting
but this thong is too tight,
these boots squeeze my brain;
cousin Bev says small sizes
take up less space in the barrel
she sends once a year.

True dem no know and ting
how down to this long hair
was paid for by the sweat
of one woman's brow:
austerity is nothing new to her.

Her whole life is a cut back
so we back home can sport
in a we khaki suit and ting.
Still she was hoping; something
about that word 'conservative'
makes her nervous.

We tell her come home
for a wash off in the sea,
a belly-full of familiar air.
Come make we give her *likkle*
bass so [she] wine up [her] waist.

She says stop the blasted styling
and singing. This is the year of corns
and calluses, extra small panties.
She is trying to buy a house;
soon love may be the only ting
she sending.

Tanya Shirley

Act

Five shillings per week for each child in a family other than the eldest

Beveridge never said
the obvious solution
was to tie your tubes;

in 1945 they understood
that the poor love kids
as much as the rich

and have the same right
to have them, the same need
to feed and clothe them

as Prime Ministers
with their afterthoughts
or Royals with coach-built prams.

Now we punish the poor
for their fecundity,
only pay for the first two

while climbing
with our Boden babies
into our 4 × 4s.

Carole Bromley

Yarl's Wood Moon

*'Just outside the window is a courtyard with a mural showing
cows and sheep grinning, as a farmer drives his tractor over the
hill to a distant purple horizon. But these are illusions. The wall
is high. The cameras stare down. The way to the outside world is
blocked, several times over'*
The Independent

Moon: cooked down like rice by lights that never go out.
Moths making radio static, interference the stars
can't get through. Just that moon. Shabby button
wearing its darkness, like everyone here – our difference
a plexiglass screen, and behind it, our moon-white guards.

Looking up at any moon is like looking down from a plane:
a dark sea that's almost familiar, an island whose one port
is a crescent of light, dirt street by the water,
place any one of us might have lived.

There's no sun. The blinds are drawn so everyone
can see the face of the TV man, the one in charge
as he says *you've got to appreciate* and *this
is a complex problem we're working on:*
words that sound learned by heart.

While he works, we're counting: up to nearly one hundred
moons. One moon cut like an onion by wires; two puddle-moons
a night-stick broke; three moons trudging the perimeter
where nothing moves. He mouths those lines many times,
blushing his blood-moon face, like a proud child.

Claire Askew

Incentivampire

from The Shapeswitching Suitboys

In daylight, he's gallant.
He hands out medallions. He says you've got talent.
Oh, Incentivampire!
He glows and he toasts like a cackling campfire.

But the longer you slave and the harder you try,
the closer he comes with his blood-hungry eye.

He seems so judicious!
His hands are as soft as the hands that do dishes,
and totally clawless.
He stands you on stage with the rest of the chorus,
says, 'You can do anything!'
He wraps you in a dark,
                                            immaculate
                                                wing.

But the longer you slave and the harder you try,
the closer he comes with his blood-hungry eye.

He throws out your crutches.
'These? You don't need them!' He takes out his matches
and melts down your glasses,
sets fire to your books and then scatters the ashes.
'I'm breaking your chains,'
he says as he skips through the blackened remains.
He's *so* big-hearted
and *so* well regarded.

But the longer you slave and the harder you try,
the closer he comes with his blood-hungry eye.

At night-time the change occurs.
He slips on his spikes and his diamond spurs
and rides into town.

He preys on the blustered and blown.
He swoops on the weak and the worked-to-the-bone.
Come morning, they're gone
and are not seen again.

And the longer you slave and the harder you try,
the closer he comes with his blood-bitter eye.

Jon Stone

Scarlet Macaws

The scarlet macaws want their red back,
not puce but rich rubescence.
They squawk and growl
for the people to give it back.

They want their green and yellow, the ultramarine
and azure of flight feathers.
They want their green homes to vibrate
against their red plumage.

They don't want to be eaten.
They don't want to be sacrificed.
They don't want to be shot for their celestial light
        and lose their eyes.
They don't want to be called Seven Macaw
        and mark the coming of the dry season
        or the hurricane season.

They don't want to be shot from the world tree
        by the Hero Twins
or be worn by them in a victory headdress.
They don't want to be bred as pets or for trade.

They want to spread their feathers
like the world's riches, a currency
that doesn't cost a thing, that doesn't
        symbolise blood.
They don't want their heads chopped off
        and stuck on poles in city temples.

They say their scarlet hue is life.
They say that every tree is an axis mundi
and all their eyes are suns.
They don't want their heads stuck on human bodies
        for funeral rites.

They don't want their ashes to treat diseases
because no medicine is left, no doctor.

They want to take their place
with the quetzal and the jaguar.
Their feathers are axes,
their feathers are lightning,
their feathers are rain

for everyone, not just the rulers with their royal aviaries.
Sun-macaws are free,
they are prayer-arrows,
Morning Stars,
they are the west wind that brings change.
They are the cardinal directions of health.

Do not bury them in human graves.
Do not bury them as plucked grave-goods
until the country is just a naked carcass
with its wings bound tight around its heart.

Pascale Petit

Memo on Council Regulations
Regarding the Little Tramp

Do not feel for the little tramp
He is bringing the hint of disorder
From some distant border
To our city doorways let's spike him
In his back and bum when
He tries to lay his weary body down
How we'll laugh at his gyrations!

Do not feed the little tramp
He'll only come back for more
Remember who the public voted for
He is perfectly capable of eating his boots
Or a fellow vagabond giant chicken
Imagine how we'll giggle at his capers –
Cannibal crunching by hypermarket bins!

Do not give cash to the Little Tramp
For scraping at a battered violin
These are austere times we are living in
And music is a frippery we can't afford
Wild crowds may gather at this fiddling
Imagine the sniggers into your sleeve
When the coppers confiscate his strings!

Do not accommodate The Little Tramp
Because you like his tender smile
Or can imagine what it's like to walk a mile
In his tongue-loose flipped-out shoes
A million others may follow in his steps
And you'd lose out on the chilling thrill
Of knocking him down with a fire-hose!

Take special care to ban him from parks
He may lay down in the flower beds
And disturb the tone of the begonias
He may pluck the lost rose of Albion
Reared with buckets of council tax
And present it between his teeth
To a blind girl who lost her benefits.
I'm sure you will agree
That we don't want that.

Andy Willoughby

I Try to Explain a Flower

to my son, who would take apart
whatever caught his eye if
I let him. Something happens
in the dark to make boldness
a necessity. Yes, the flower is
saying something somehow,
and we must let it. Heartfelt.
It means the heart has little
hands and pats its pockets
like Daddy when he's trying
to remember where he put
whatever it is he was supposed to
keep close. Yes, money most
of the time, or time, or keys
to home. No, you don't need
one to open a flower. Money
is beautiful, in a way. Like lots
of things we might not see
for seeing all the time, or don't
see but dream of. Dreaming
is a kind of worry, yes, and a
flower, happening as it does
in the dark. Someone knows
why, but not Daddy. Don't
touch. You can feel by looking.
Then we'll do something.

Jacob Polley

First Word

'Bye,' he says, already awake. He means, 'Hello.'

'Bye,' he says, his first word of the day, the first word of his life.
'Bye,' he says, meaning 'Hi! Hello!'
The house trembles with his tiny, wrong-way-round greeting.
In the animation of this story his dream creatures will understand –
                                     he is entering human waking time now,
people creatures are forced to thrive in daylight,
to dream with their conscious bodies,
he has to leave his companions now.
'Bye' means 'Hello' in our world
but 'See you tonight,' to his night-time friends.

'Bye,' he says, warning his daytime keepers gently, rouse yourselves now,
I've let my darkness go, dismiss yours. There's work to do here.
They acknowledge the command, each turning away from each,
mumbling, 'It's your turn, isn't it?' until one of them submits.

'Bye,' he says, a little later in the morning,
turning around in his umpire's chair,
                                   tensing his harness, leaning towards his mother,
'Bye,' his mother says, breezily, as if breezily.

He is not an umpire he is a judge,
puritanical like a newspaper. He is greedy (like a newspaper).
'Bye,' his mother says, brightly, 'Bye,' she says again, smiling, determined.
He waves his hand. It is a few weeks before he will sob at such departures.

'Bye,' he says, this morning alone with his father.
There is a commotion in the turquoise field
but the synthetic animals, yes, have resolved the issue,
there's a challenge every day on children's TV.

'Bye,' he says, this morning alone with his father.
There is a commotion in the red and blue field.
The synthetic animals can't resolve the issue.
There's a challenge every day on Breakfast News.

('Bye,' his father once said, to Scotland in the abstract,
                    when more than half of that territory's people
voted themselves into a region – openly, finally, willed themselves a satellite
of Westminster.

His father that morning was lecturing him, on plug sockets and politics.
'They say the well-to-do gave their country away –
those who said 'No thanks' to their own country,
'Bye,' to their own country,
had already enjoyed free education, a free health service,
who cares if their grandchildren wouldn't have that privilege,
younger folks have to learn to fend for themselves.
The 'No thanks' were Edinburgh devotees of a bit of peace-and-quiet,
            they saw nuclear slaughter on the Clyde as 'No great mischief,'
they were the keep-it-in-the-family spoon-in-the-mouthers,
the Comfortable in the countryside, the Satisfied in the suburbs,
pep-talk rugger leaders,
they were the professional moral-high-grounders,
content for decades, they said, to be the UK's conscience,
as long as their vote changed nothing.

'They must have practiced for the Referendum –
quietly, patiently –
perhaps they employed private tutors –
perfecting the lifting of the Ballot Biro.
In some places it was a flimsy pencil, the kind Ikea supply
for do-it-yourself projects,
but the 'No thanks' folks are unfamiliar with do-it-yourself
at a political level –
why bother if Britain already does everything for you,
and what if you got a skelf?
You have to be careful – 'No thanks' people make a little god of Careful –
so they practiced and practiced.
In some places it was with a flimsy pen,
the kind boys and girls force into the electricity supply
                    when no one else is looking,
the kind the Lotto provides in newsagents for hope upon hope
but the 'No thanks' have no need for wild vulnerable hope, they've been

investing primly for years,
>their financial advisors tell them,
the Tip Top British Companies tell them,
the British we're-not-nationalists tell them, play safe
(play safe is appropriate for infants, son)
(don't call us nationalists, the British national Labour Party says),
and the No Thanks are experts now, experts of thou shalt not,
experts of scare,
they have UK state-funded doctorates in No –
'No! No! No!', Thatcher's favourite triad
has surely been improved by them,
with puritanical minimalism you now only have to say it once,
but look, they have
>calluses on their hands,
muscular pain in their arms and backs –
and the little pencils and pens have joined together,
formed ladder after ladder,
gained density, immense weight.
As they know, it's hard work pulling a ladder up behind you,
>and the health service that had helped them hoard hope to
themselves
may not help them so readily in the new Britain they have approved.)

'Bye,' the boy says to his father, quietly, gently,
(the softness of an infant's voice)
meaning it's fine to be high on bitterness – for a few moments, it's fine,
even, to be unfair –
but when I could barely crawl you warned me
come away from the meeting of the wall and the door,
watch your fingers as the door finally opens, have faith, the door is
finally opening,
and now his father wants to change the subject,
is saying almost without conviction,
'You do know Scotland has just become a satellite from the 1950s
and London has a weapon –
it can remove space junk by remote control.'

'Bye,' the boy says mindfully at the child-minder's,
as his aunty lifts him up from the ruins,
                                        the lettered bricks on Lina's
scrupulous floor.
No tower of words yet,
no 'Ciao' for the moment, except from Lina, who says 'Bye,' as well.

'Bye,' he says, turning around in his life-guard's chair,
                                tensing his harness, leaning towards his father,
smiling quietly and now waving broadly with one tiny hand.
'Bye,' he says, 'Bye.'

'Bye,' the father's mother says, meaning cheerio, meaning take care,
sweetheart
(he's a teenager and she still calls him sweetheart,
he's a teenager and now he's decades older
but in this story she's somehow alive)
Did you pick up the new tea bread? – I've wrapped it in a clean tea towel,
                                it's in the Quality Street tin.
'Bye,' she says every Sunday on his own personalised, glimpsey, tv channel,
Troubling Nostalgia,
'Tea-bread is 'brain-food', I read an article about it.'
Bye,' she says, with that old sweeties tin now in her hands, making sure he
takes it,
with its aromatic tea bread and unfolding tapestry of the butterflies of
England.
They call sweets swedgers here, Mum.

'Bye,' the father's father says, meaning goodbye boys, grownup boys,
                                here's to America and forgetting,
let me forget, you can live too long, let me find warmth, you can't grow old
in America.

'Bye,' the father's father says, twenty-five years later, in poverty, in Florida,
secretly selling his father's carpentry tools from the 1920s
for the next meal at Subway,
you can live too long, you can't find warmth, human warmth, you can't
grow old in America,
America is coming your way.

Enough of Troubling Nostalgia, it's not a high value package,
the reception is always poor.

'Bye,' the wee guy says, to his own infant miracles –
he'll remember nothing of his first steps trying to walk through the
flatscreen,
into the world of television,
of the demonization of every collective endeavour except hush hush
privilege,
its self-special 'all-in-this-together' misdirection,
nothing of his high-vis training shoes,
                yellow-and-blue with laces-shy Velcro, bringing them to his father
as a puppy mumbles a lead in its mouth, padding up to its owner,
asking her now can we go walking?
'Bye,' the boy says, his last word of the day,
a small beach where language will set off for the next island, the moon,
and the next island, Mars, where there are already new forms of the old
language and island and island and island of planets,
                ranging, stretching out, sharp ancient islands,
far out in the space
sea,
islands to be populated, diminishing,
finally,

                                                to a last skerry, a last
just-concealed rock, the future of murmur, a single faint whisper,
and a voice still saying 'Bye' and meaning 'Hello.'

Richard Price

the summer of

that was the summer they didn't write their books
Ink was cheap but they were looking for work
that was the summer the plays didn't get booked
no one was in the mood to play
and the tickets
that summer no one went to the beach
except of course some people did
and no one went and sat in the lush green shade of the countryside
even though the countryside is free
(for now) because of the train fare
and the importance of
looking for work
that summer the diy shops went out of business
you either had money to get the builders in
or you were trying to hang
pick one: the wallpaper, on by your teeth, yourself
that summer no one opened the post
that summer no passport was post-haste eviction
notice
all over Europe the borders went up and the boats went down
it was portcullis weather
it was beach whether
portcullis or passport
that summer we all went abseiling without leaving the comfort of
that summer it was extreme sports all right and it was extreme
art
the art of
that summer they were en plein air, their
easels, cooking pots and baby things
spread out under the blue moon.

Katy Evans-Bush

To Dream of Copper Denotes Oppression from Those above You in Station

after Gustavus Hindman Miller's Dictionary of Dreams

Your dream denotes sorrow and vexation.
Some deceitful person has installed himself at the heights of prosperity.
Unhappy conditions are piled thick around you.
Enemies are circulating detrimental reports.

Your dreams are abandoned.
They are abandoned in that you will have difficulty framing your plans for future success.
Little sustenance will be eked out by your own labours.
You will suffer for another's wild folly.

No good will come from this dream.
It foretells an event will cast a sickening fear of living around you.
You will find yourself tangled in meshes of perplexity; the victim of nervous troubles.
A withering state of things bodes no well for the dreamer.

Your dream is significant of a chronic stage.
Enemies will chase your every effort, you will suffer exasperating gloom.
Loss will be added to unconquerable griefs.
After a season of disquiet, public rioting will follow.

Your dream is not always a bad dream.
It signifies opposition to enemies' workings against you.
If you dream your sympathies are enlisted for the sorrows of others
                              – true friends will attend you.
Those in power will lose.

Amy Key

Go Not, Gentle

I loved Hope. Born in the rain of the First of April
Two Thousand Eleven, she cowered with her sturdy mother
and sister against the lichened wall, till
brought to be dry and safe in the barn.

Yet a crowd of London gawkers blundered in.
Afterwards, feeding an orphan, I heard
a cry, saw Hope too needed to be fed.

Rejected now by her mother she sickened, her eye
flared. The vets tried. But by next day
the blood was running down her face.

Gathering her up in my arms, I fed her first.
'Enucleate' was the word they used on the bill.
I nursed her as the sewn lids healed.

I chased her through the fields in sun and snow.
She hurled herself against me then at the milk.

She was always small – didn't lamb with her sisters,
but she had a tup at three, then at four a ewe.

She called to me over the fields, and daily
trundled over, nuzzled my hand for food,

trailing her lamb along. Then I found her dead.
Her lamb cries still.

I named her Gentle. I have marked her wool:
when the other lambs go to be sold at market,

she will stay.

Josephine Dickinson

Deathfall

Before Koni, before Museveni, before Obote's second term,
before now there was me. We were in deep shit! Bridges couldn't be fixed
with gaffer-tape. America stopped lending plasticine to fill pot-holes.
I quit playing refugee. Who among you was going to pay our country's
light bill? Well? You uninvited guests like Rome, you will know where
we put the bodies in their tunics and kangas. My sins, both real and imagined,
into the trap. To my brother my rival, when he comes don't let him tap
the glass (idiots), devise his death. You stable-god, a month's worth
of grain for the paratroop regiment won't purge you.

New wives and shoes and a move to State House while we live in huts.
Home will see your troubles cursed. By the way, your Chief of Police,
into the trap. You who believed in Churchill's prophecy. You innocents
ruled by a spinning earth, your tears will quench the barns we set fire to.
You who call your guns She. You papier mâché martyrs
with north Kiboko accents. You shadow soldiers who dig dead men
from their graves. You in the motion of battle. You who search the airwaves
for the British World Service, who stare spirits in the face
but can't stand heights, the rules say, into the trap.

I will not forgive the clan who sheds blood for party politics.
Your god might. The one with his hands up as he waves, ask the firing squad
to send him with the widowers, orphans and motherless sons, into the trap.
All you disciples of empires. Mr Men ministers who paraphrase over
PA systems, into the trap. Wrecked after five days of being held
under decree nineteen. Why riffle through your Yellow pages in search
of Heads-of-state? Into the trap. The executioner who lets you watch
his navel after bare-knuckle fights, into the trap. You who played
The Bard on screen and stage, or quoted Aristotle, into the trap.

Your second tongue, into the trap. Lumino-boy with that Yankee
dialect, into the trap. It makes no difference to me, you sun worshiper.
Name your Icarus and fly, into the trap. You who abandon
your wife's thighs for the cradle of a servant girl, into the trap.
You at The Uganda Company Limited (Trojans), because you gave us
cotton but took our land, follow me with your horse mask,
into the trap. Those who offer me your skins as a fig leaf, let me carve
a map on your backs to Ithaca. You can hitchhike for all I care:
into the trap. Take your stand with the soothsayer in her snake dress.
The ones who hesitate: into the trap.

Nick Makoha

Once Upon A Time

Once upon a time there was the water
Where was it?
On the edge of the water
Where it reaches land
Where did you say?
Where the water reaches land
Whose then?
Where our water becomes our land, you mean
Where our water is our land and our sand is our sand
That's where it was
The way it lay there
The way it lay face down, just so, the hands beside the head
The way we removed it and it stayed lying face down
Even when we removed it, it stayed, while we were removing
it, lying face down in the sand
Even when we were no longer looking
Especially where we were no longer looking it stayed lying in
the sand, face down
That it one day would leave by itself, we sometimes thought,
But that it would become ours when we removed it
We knew
Once upon a time, we still tried to think, but
As loud as we could tried once upon a time, to keep thinking
once upon a time

Peter Verhelst
Translation by Willem Groenewegen

Inyenzi

*'They had become people to throw away. They were no longer
what they had been, and neither were we.'*
Génocidaire Ignace Rukiramacumu,
interviewed in Jean Hatzfeld, *A Time for Machetes:
The Rwandan Genocide – The Killers Speak.*

Beveridge was insane.

He genetically engineered
a race of shape-shifting cockroaches
walking on hind-legs
like uppity pigs.

He clothed them in trackies and baseball caps,
wigged them in gel and hi-tensile scrunchies.

Nutrition was important:
they thrived on chips   and heroin

proliferating

in fried food, sweat
and cigarette hutches   grease.

They were repulsive:
some grotesquely corpulent,
others skeletal on crack;
Special Brew shrunk some skulls reptilian.
They were toothless and hairless,
pimpled in blackheads and shiny with pus.

Nevertheless
they seemed to find each other attractive
mating continually and without compunction.
Even the juveniles were fertile,
farrowing in nests of shredded garbage
in plasma-screened council dens.

Presently, they became a problem.
They were an aesthetic blight.
They burgled our houses
and were prone to raping or murdering their children.
But mostly they took advantage of our charity,
their appetite for consumption
matched only by their aversion to work.
And everything was always
someone else's fault – or responsibility –
they would not help themselves.

Misguided people from the churches,
looked down on their squalor
and felt sympathy, arguing passionately
that, 'something should be done'
to ameliorate their 'plight':
e.g. lots more free stuff they'd done nothing to deserve;
houses, hospitals, social-care, training –
hope for a better life.

But of course, they had forgotten:
they were only cockroaches,
walking on hind-legs   pigs

Steve Ely

The Garden is Not for Everyone

All summer the children have been running **in the global refugee crisis**
in the communal garden **Ammar is searching for his brother on a train**
kicking a football through the yellow roses, chasing **the bodies roll out**
across the parched ground **on the platform, a woman lifts a card sign**
I hear their cries from the fourth floor **help us, save our souls! A child**
on my side of the block & some days **who looks like my child is asleep**
I take my boy down there to play **in the calm waters of a tourist beach**
with Luna's boys – Albert, Adam, Ali, **the newspapers don't know how**
they live on the council side. Luna is Ethiopian I think **this story ends**
and I mean to ask when I see her down on our street **but describe the**
baby bound in batik on her chest, but instead **smell of 71 people dead**
we talk about the letter in her mailbox: **in a truck on the highway. We**
the council children can no longer use **sincerely wish we could help**
the communal garden – there is no reason **in the global refugee crisis**.

Hannah Lowe

The Bus Riders' Creed

We believe that passengers, like motorists, are people
who need to move from one place to another;
that if their destination is too far for them to walk,
they should have provided safe,
efficient means to get them there;
that these means are more efficient shared, and that sharing,
as every toddler knows, is good;
that therefore it is no imposition to take yourself to a public
stop, and wait with other passengers;
nor is it an infringement of your rights to have to wait for
transport while it pauses at other people's stops;
that everyone who can pay pays the same price for the same
distance, and those who can't pay should be helped to pay;
that those who need help to get on should be helped to get on,
and if other passengers can help them, then they should;
that if someone needs your seat more than you do, then you
should stand;
that it is permissible, if there is room, for you to place
your stuff beside you on another seat, but if that seat
is then required by another passenger, you should
pick up your stuff and let the other person sit, because stuff
is neither in nor of itself important;
that the woman with the walking frame moving ever so
ever so slowly onto the bus and down the aisle deserves your
patience, because you would need it in her
place, and one day, probably, you will;
that all the boys and girls who shout into their phones and at
each other deserve your tolerance, because they are young
and having their turn;
that small, friendly children deserve a smile back;
that small, wailing children deserve compassion, and so do
their parents;
that as long you are on the bus, the other passengers are
putting up with you as well, and you should remember that;

that in one life you will be many different passengers;
that they know nothing worth the knowing,
who travel only in cars.

Joanne Limburg

Mr. Duncan-Smith Dreaming in the Sun

A man is knocking down a high brick wall
only to rebuild it further from the swollen river,
each brick re-finding its original neighbour,
the wall somehow more massive than before.

Torrential rain from a bright sky,
though the ground is bone.
Days of rain upon the man and the wall in minutes
make him pace back and forth and change tack.

Now he is smashing the bricks, bagging the bits,
piling the bags in a line, then a stack, then, well, a wall.
The water laps against the bags, soaks them dull.
The earth is a footprint set hard and sharp.

There are children up on roofs, arms out,
shadowing helicopters and planes,
smudge-faced children down in the dirt
scratching for tools of make believe.

There are parents looking for their children,
good parents looking for naughty and nice alike.
The motives of others, says the voiceover,
the unfathomable motives of others.

Mark Robinson

Calais

This mud is different.
Were I writing home
I'd struggle to describe
its darker pigment,
how it slips beneath our feet,
a long, slow slide
where boots lose grip.

Under our sheeting
we listen to the rain;
traffic on the near road
lets out a groan, a hiss.
We have learned the art
of slow patience,
of being still endlessly.

There is always tomorrow,
always the chance
that there will be movement.
Today we cheered
when someone's phone
showed a man walking
out of a tunnel's darkness.

Nicholas Murray

Llanddeusant

The chapel crouches slack,
broken backed on the verge wall.
Too many years of sky sinking
stone. Cloud weight.

Behind, Carmarthen Fan climbs
with low swollen mounds
before a shear crag wall
of tooth toppled sandstone.

Mid Wales recumbent.
A lane winds in past the last lonely farm,
bounding over the parish like the band
around a tennis ball.

The whole world is backed away
to those who shut doors
on everything but the land, seeing
more clearly than anyone that here lies their raft.

Night. And the stone rent valley
syncopates the sparkling
of the filter brook to the crowding
eye-winks of a thousand watching stars.

Morning. The clouds are tower
stacked, ashen demolitions rising
from the south as though the colliers'
cottage fires, valley hidden, still burned.

Paul Deaton

Untitled

We were desperate for something authentically fake to believe in.
The Baptist blew in from the desert: sometimes in shirtsleeves,
sometimes in hard hat, sometimes in hygienic hairnet,
aspirating 'bout 'ha-ha-haspiration', tumbleweed mumbling
of one-nation-building, 'ha-ha-having a go, taking a risk, ha-ha-having
a punt'. Why do you pump me up (*pump me up*) buttercup, baby,
just to let me down? Salome breezed into town with a brace
of hand-me-down veils snatched from the polling station jumble sale,
auditioned her sword dance for Britain's Got Talons,
struck a deal with The Baptist and left him intact with
his shirtsleeves, his hairnet and hygienic hard hat.

Simon Barraclough

Ministry
of Peace

Security

Trick or Treaters are not all kids as
campers are not all happy and I wish
the banks would just start lending or
improve their customer service you know
I have to use a plastic keypad just to
check my balance which is invaluable
in the fight against fraud so when
you bowled towards me outside Bank
in the costume of the dead that is to say
masked and painted I had to ask the value
of that feint of pure hostility you are
clearly having fun which is a good thing
don't let me stop you

on my island none of this would be true

Tom Chivers

Preferendum

1979, 1997, 2014, 201…

Ochone a rí, ochone a rí,
it's the time has come for the grand telling…..

Sit down, haud furrit, cock a lug to me
in Dumfries, in Dingwall, in Dores & Dundee,
in Australia, New Zealand, the US of A,
feel the tide of an old freedom swelling.

Gather the remnants from king to collective,
rip up the plaids of the past thousand years,
shake off the stoor that'd blind you forever
& wipe off your jockodile tears.

Ochone a rí…..call a by to the moaning
& puke out the language that gies us the boak,
cough up the shackles that weigh down the race,
rid your harns of the legends that smother this place,
that've grown more important than folk.

Cock a lug to the swirl of the kilts & the drums,
to the snash of the factories & belch of the lums
& remember, our 'betters' would rather the clan
of one brain than one free thinking woman or man.

Puke out the language & gralloch the sounds
of the clanking old shackles still weighing us down.
Once & for all take a look at the lot
we've been sold to console us & make us The Scots.

The mist, the midges, cockade & claymore,
Gordonstoun, Loch Lomond, Braemar,
haggis, neeps, the Wee Free Kirk,
a wedding kilt with a plastic dirk,
Holyrood, Mon's Meg, Glamis & Cawdor,
Rangers, Celtic, Harry Lauder,
Culloden, Flodden, Prestonpans,
the wee white rose, the Drunk Man,
the working man, The Vow & Labour,
whisky, woad & michty cabers,
The Monarch of the Heathery Glen,
the lassies, rashes, lochs & bens,
The Corries, porridge, Brigadoon,
Rob Roy, Braveheart & The Broons,
The Tartan Army, qualifying,
thinking, drinking, not qualifying.

Aly Bain & Norman MacCaig
Gartcosh, Seafield, Ravenscraig
Wattie Scott, Rab Burns, Will Fyffe
Murphy, Darling, Brown, Forsyth
Dr. Findlay, Para Handy
Yarrow, Fairfield & Ferranti
Bonnie Prince Charlie, the Silvery Tay
Torness, Corpach&Dounreay
Highland Marys & Missus Macks,
Tie ups, Trident, Bedroom Tax
The Big Yin, Still Game, Frankie Boyle
The Barnett Formula, North Sea oil
Maxton, Gallacher, Maclean
100,000 hungry weans
The Daily Record – Scotland's Winner!
& so the lines get longer, thinner.....

New road extensions bypass schemes,
McDonalds, Poundworlds, blues & greens
that don't belong this side of Ireland,
islands now no longer islands,
Auld Reekie, Festival & Fringe,
a dearth of trawlers on the Minch
& families in port and town
with less than nocht to go around
sit cowered before the foreign telly
ignoring rumbling, empty bellies.....

Rip up the postcards, the tea towels & place-mats,
empty the biscuit tins, flambé the scones,
burst open, break down & demolish the walls
& the yetts& the towers & splendiferous halls
of the crumbling, ancestral old pile we call home.

We're canny, no cannae, we're aye and we're *aye*,
we're Scottish, we're British, we're World, we're I.
The bullet of hope fired into a box,
the bomb of the future explodes in a cross.

Stuart A. Paterson

no change given

the news is no less shit
when wrapped in sun

the taste of loss still
sour as an unripe plum

a hemisphere can't shift
the weight of death

or else of dying
hope face down

& drowned again
in puddles of infernal

spring & me still waiting
on lenin's slow train

alone & forlorn & in
the grip of northern rain

april's thesis
still unproclaimed

jerusalem postponed
our flags left maimed

no chink of paltry light
to grace our days

all vigour subjected
to unspecified delays

Paul Summers

The Promised Land

It's in the nature of a promised land
that you won't reach it. From the shadeless plains,
oppressed by rulers and their merchant friends,

bereaved by wild dogs and scorpions,
you lurch, whole villages of thwarted wrath,
the sick on mules to give them half a chance,

towards a narrow spur, its tiny grove
where green figs and the water prove your road.
You scale the high couloir, and build stone graves

where children fall or sickness shrinks your load
and by this shaming is your grief annealed:
to lose the weak is tinged with gratitude;

and so you swear, at the edge of a bare wold,
again, to make this journey from a state
of shuttered plenty to an even fold

rich men can scorn and cart their booty out
but may not rule, since you, the people, made
this journey on this date. The way is tight,

and spearmen in the heights leave many dead
as you press through the pass that stretches far
into and through extremities of need;

starvation kills as many and the sores
of grisly plagues confirm that beauty's not
essential to the ways of righteousness.

Our Gods! Our Gods! The convoy quops with fright.
A false Messiah works the troubled line
with rumours of a giant strix that waits

beyond the mountains in your dreams' domain.
Your feet are yielding and the sky is doubt;
six panniers of cheese have lost their brine.

Just then a cry goes up: the furthest scout
has reached the edge of this incessant chain
and seen the way. It is an anguished shout.

what lies below is not the coastal scene
arrayed with vines and creels of winking squid
you had imagined but another plain

as sere and sharpened as the one you fled.
A yellow wolf already teases near.
This land will take some work to make it good;

but even as you gather round to hear
each other's counsel, others turn to go
back through the pass towards the waiting fires

the vengeful rulers there have lit. The you
that was a multitude is now at large
across the slopes of sage and weeping through

this last free night before the homeward march
to servitude and home worse than before:
the evil road, the shame-remembered gulch

and then the plain, where waits the rulers' fire.
From this lone height you watch the darkened gulf
and learn what happens when, as happened here,

a people breaks its promise to itself.

Tony Williams

The Ballad of the Ship's Captain

*'What would happen if someone were to choose the captains of
ships by their wealth, refusing to entrust the ship to a poor
person even if he was a better captain?
They would make a poor voyage of it.'*
from a conversation between Plato, Socrates and Adeimantus
in *The Republic*

The ship itself had been in good shape,
but oh my love, the new Captain. The new Captain
came aboard in a ticker tape swarm,
and I'd swear it's ermine he was wrapped in.

The ship itself had had a decent crew.
They'd pulled together for years. For years
their course had been reasonably true, through storm
and war and hunger and fears

but the Captain, the Captain was a high, proud man
chosen on account of his wealth. His wealth,
my love, was his master plan. He cared
nothing for crew, or their welfare and health.

His only concern? That the ship travelled faster,
that the crew was kept in its place. Its place
was enforced, as slaves to a master, with bared
steel and guns, bandied close to the face.

It was mutiny, mutiny, played out back to front
by a man who'd never suffered the sea. The sea
ate his sense; we felt the brunt. The hair triggers
of a sociopath's glee.

The Captain, the Captain, brought in his lawyers
to manage stores, navigation, the rig. The rig
became rotten after sawyers and riggers
dissented and were thrown in the brig

The Captain, the Captain, just didn't give a damn.
The trickle-down we got was salt water. Salt water
isn't something you should cram into mouths
unless you intend a slow slaughter.

It didn't matter in the end. The ship ran aground
on an island unseen by the lawyers. The lawyers
who'd argued for three different souths,
not one of which was their employer's.

The Captain, the Captain, drowned with his gold,
frothing and crying and swearing. And, swearing
allegiance to each other in the hold, we paddled
to the shore; survived by scrimping and sharing.

But the Captain, my love, he had many heirs
and rich men who followed his lead. His lead
was idiotic, left our affairs saddled
in thrall to the thrill of his greed.

These Captains, these Captains know little else
but boarding school's compassionless bite. Less bite,
and more brute; tightening our belts not theirs.
A fine way of picking a fight.

Whether leading a nation or a ship on the seas
a Captain should be bound by a tether. A tether
to the many, not plutocracy's heirs,
so we're truly all in this together.

Adam Horovitz

7/5/2015 In this class

let's be clear (1) how I swung from the frayed
end of a Tory line through boarding schools
and into university at seventeen

that (2) my tutor took one look and passed me
de Beauvoir Fanon Tsvetaeva (3) ensuring
I would never be an army wife though being of the thieving

bourgeoisie I have her copies still (4)
in my own university room so temperate and light
and not unlike in many ways an Officers' Mess lunch

(5) but for being filled in riptides with your kids
who may or may not know freedom from disaster
or be up all night on highs or the thick unreadable

dread I rode at their age having just cast votes (6)
over Homer v. the bar we're at the bar discussing
voice how voice is always elsewhere something

one must find and lay alongside like a bearskin i.e.
rarely native or a sweet fit or indeed the animal
one thought one was but (7) try it on I say in one

way or another daily it's a trouble and a right
and (8) they do they will just keep on speaking up
your kids who by the way are ok are magnificent

Tiffany Atkinson

Today

I had drunk so much coffee I was shivering as if something
inside of me was about to go off I stopped to stare
out of the window watched a plane fly over so loud it frightened me
reminded me of the fear of a nuclear attack which is as real to me
now as it was when I was a child

the phone rings telling me I can get solar panels and later another
about a new boiler paid for by the government the government.
the one that doesn't care about people dying from poverty
and humiliation old people who are starving can't heat their homes
single mothers who have no one to look after their children

while they are working unable to progress past sixteen hours
people with learning difficulties whose families can't cope with them
at home with no break the nurses who get paid less than politicians
girls working in shops and cafes on the minimum wage who can't afford
a house men in low paid jobs who are told be grateful so they go home

feeling small it's always the children who suffer my husband comes home
doesn't ask how I am disappears upstairs keeps busy the washing still out
on the line in the rain for three days but in three days things will have changed
again I might be in a better mood I might not be scared of a nuclear attack
or worry about all the things in the world that I cannot change.

Arwen Webb

Deep

Be a Miner. Because Britain Will Always Need Coal
National Coal Board advertisement, 1970s

Nineteen eighty-four, eighty-five.
They knew austerity long before
we did. An uncivil war.
They had to dig deep to survive.
Their fears have been proved right:
*Close the pit and you might
as well put a sign at the school that says
DOLE OFFICE – THIS WAY*.
But it was all such a long time ago.
Orgreave isn't Hillsborough, or so
it's claimed. Let sleeping
slag heaps lie. Let the grass grow.
Let puzzled children ask the meaning
of the word *colliery*.

Two hundred then. Now just three:
Thoresby, Hatfield, Kellingley.
And soon there'll be none.
Thatcher called them *the enemy within*:
now, their last battalion
surrenders its arms. Let wheels spin,
and cable loop around its drum;
bring them to the surface, blinking
at the unforgiving light.
Chain the gates behind them,
watch them walk away from history,
into a country others voted for.
Maggie has her final victory,
and no one needs to dig deep any more.

Alan Buckley

Scotland's Hidden Gems

In the hotel here there's a painting
of Eilean Donan Castle,
as if that merciless piece of touristry
had been transported to the Rain Forest.
Huge spoons of leaves loll round the eyes
as you peer through lush and savage trees.
Though by an amateur it is a work of genius,
and how I long to see her other work:
the Scott Monument in the Marianas Trench,
furred by barnacles and only occasionally
illuminated by electric fish;
Balmoral on the surface of the sun;
the Duke of Sutherland's statue
inverted down some giant toilet bowl.
I'm not the artist, but I'd call the series
Scotland's Hidden Gems.

Hugh McMillan

Ghazal

is the Human Rights Act in the desert *Inshallah*
are Freedom of Speech and Equal Ops
curlews in the crazy desert *Inshallah*

repetition of treasures in the Congo
repetition of bobble heads across poppy valleys

does the Kaaba glow on the road to Raqqa *Inshallah*
what swollen pass must these sandals tread
for the scar of Jerusalem *Inshallah*

repetition of warriors on the Screen of Thrills repetition
where I'm swung in love with a gun aboard my back

who has taken my house and eats my bread *Inshallah*
who takes the pen from the head so its flesh
harden to a vessel of God in muezzin cry *Inshallah*

repetition of robots in the sky repetition of babies blown
like dolls in a market repetition of fresh torn martyrs

why are my daughters in the desert *O Inshallah*
for the theft of the word where one man's Allah
is beheaded by one man's Allah for *Inshallah*

Daljit Nagra

farfalla

migration season
the trade winds turn
blowing north

up across
the blue eye'd
mediterrancan

that middle passage
whose depths are
seeded with bones

ship graves,
their hulls stream
with tidal veils

as on rescue boats
uniformed sailors oil
their gun sights

a closed
blue door
to meet them

the old greeting
for returning
ghosts

Morgan Downie

The Muse in the market place

In the Neo-liberal world
A dog with a collar crosses
The road at the zebra lines.

The vernacular was never its surrogate womb
This poem was not conceived with translation in mind
Will never let itself be adopted
Or exported to worldwide markets
Nor will the metaphors mellow down
To make it amenable to translation
Into an alien tongue.

This poem refuses to undergo painful procedures
Like the long intrusive questionnaire
Cleansing its tracts
Before it is granted a visa
To be read at international festivals.

To be frisked
Through its taut contours
Of line breaks and paragraphs
At airports and check points
With every image bent like a question mark
In ludicrous submission.

Chandramohan S

To My God-daughter

August 2015

I kiss my god-daughter on the forehead
and sitting underneath
the light blue of a Tory sky
tell her slowly

that not even the air we breathe –
though we might own it for
a second as it passes through
our lungs – is really ours.

I tell her to renounce possession.
In cities like our own,
the price of free movement
is always being alone.

I tell her not to do what men say,
but open to the breeze
as clouds are on a given day
become a congeries.

Above us, armies clash by night,
cloud-shaped drones
or drone-shaped clouds circling
the prow of a lifeboat.

In the lowest rung of the troposphere,
a billion invisible
droplets clump together,
darken and fall.

Will Harris

There is a bigger telling that moves around the world

In Britain   rain like newsprint   the poor getting poorer   something
that might have been done   was not done   and the cold no of it echoes.

On site   builders   in their bright hats   digging drilling lifting building
muscles flexing   relaxing   in Paleolithic   rhythm.

And shouting!   they must shout   above the noise of the rain
above pneumatic pounding   and the clang of spades   opening the ground.

Here in Oz   sun centre-spreads the sky's backdrop   to our backyard bbq
radio buzzing   with stories of asylum seekers   denied asylum.

The humble muscles of our tongues   flake words like flint
into the afternoon   words that sinter   into the tumulus of understanding

that will be mounded over us.   We know that all we have   is because of
mistake   cellular mishaps   accidents   of birth   the taking and taking

history's cruelties   secreted in the earth.   But over by the barbie
someone is helping a child   flip the meat   passing a metal spatula

saying 'spatula'   and when the child says 'badala'   'that's right, spatula.'
There is a song of yes   in our blood   the ultimate thump-thump of it.

The unkindnesses that happen   are not the last thing   that will happen.
We have all the words   and we'll use them   just see how we will.

Alison Flett

Island

You close your eyes and there they are:
dark eyed, brimming with language.
They press with languid babes-in-arms
against the railings you've erected
with your handfuls of nails and your
nightmarish effort. You sweat and weep
against their will to be remembered.
They fill the dirty sea of your brain
with their boats, cry out at the edge
of your imaginings, making you angry.
The island is your state of grace.
With your child and your husband
you live inside a square of time
that you painstakingly unrolled,
mended, embroidered and defined.
You can't survive without this space.
You spend your days pacing its borders.
Now they are smuggling themselves in.
You wake to screaming and banging.
Each star is a tiny searchlight,
and you know the time has come.
You bring your husband and your child
down to the sea that whispers home.
It's a matter of win or be won.
It's breath or suffocation.

Polly Clark

Ministry
of Plenty

Another Shift

Back to back, our chair wheels locking in a way
that makes us secretly hate our neighbour.
We swivel and watch the clock as if
we were whippets waiting for the bell.
The belts feed us lines of everyone's potatoes,
sanitary towels, scented candles, meat.

Every time I touch the cold of a haunch of pork
I want to clean myself. – I can feel the juices
of its smelly death. Sticky, like I had a juicy peach
with a side of horror. Un-lickable. I feel
the parasites of salmonella crawl my arms;
smile, remember to sell the saving stamps
that suck in the poor. Catch their Christmas
even though it's only May.

People complain about carrier bags – that they split
around boxes of bran flakes, let out the apples. Vodka
is always on offer – ditto the whisky and gin.
Keep them pissed – locked in their worlds
of local argument. We hate it here – every one of us
missing our children's milestones, swapping our joy
for minimum wage. We buy back our bit
of motherly love in ounces of fizz-bombs. We hope

our sons and daughters think of us as they suck on sugar –
hope their mouths make a memory of us in the chewing.
We buy our guilt in grams and sigh at next week's rota –
tell each other little stories of our lives, smooth
the bunches in our uniforms.
Whenever we have the chance,
we wash our hands.

Jane Burn

The Blue Queen of Ashtrayland

'What the fuck's the Holy Grail?'
Molly in *Urban Grimshaw and the Shed Crew*

Her hair glows, burnished as the gold
that trims her Nike cardigan;
Ionian white her Fila trainers,
DKNY jeans and cap.

Her skin's as blue as old skimmed milk;
as blue the star on her left cheek
a Borstal beauty spot, tattooed
with broken glass and laundry ink.

The downers downed, the brown all tooted,
the homegrown hydroponic skunk
all shotgunned, blown-back, jointed, bonged,
the Queen calls for her royal Swan.

Through snakebite piercings on her lips
the bitten red adaptor hissed
like Cleopatra's asp its gas.
Our Queen jerks upright, claps her hands.

With no round table, they hand round
White Lightning in two-litre flasks.
She necks a draught then kicks her minstrel:
Skeeter fills the block with song,

'Bring me my Dig of burning gold,
Bring me Viagra of desire!
Bring me my foil: O, clouds unfold!
Bring me my Milligrams of Fire!'

Her knights take off to rob a dealer.
Urban's passed out on his crate.
Peeling back a cardboard curtain,
their Queen looks down on her estate.

Ian Duhig

The sixth verse quotes Skeeter's song from Bernard Hare's *Urban Grimshaw and The Shed Crew* (Sceptre 2006), his account of a particularly marginalised Leeds gang of school and social dropouts. 'Ashtrayland' is Urban's name in the book for an England whose history, politics and culture are remote from and irrelevant to the Shed Crew's lives, a mirror-image of the views expressed by Conservative MP Mark Garnier, who in 2014 referred to 'dog-end voters' living in 'the outlying regions of Britain' with whom his party need not concern itself.

The Smell of the Suburbs

This bank's inside beats to the beep
of the ATM keyed outdoors. Lunchtimers clutch
waste-lidded cups, fickle through traffic
to lean into their long unpensioned deaths
quietly strangled by lanyards.
An empty bus squeals past spilled
old bins, hacked-back rhubarb
writhes with stems. At the wheel
a driver inhales diesel and vomit-sweet
fumes. A quince bursts pink,
riots the rain, unreported.

Beth McDonough

The Maid of Norway Window,
Lerwick Town Hall

Softness itself, the fair hair loose,
flowing over fur, the childish curve
of the cheek. And metal: one crown
heavy on the small head, her hands
full of another. Her cloak clasped
with a gold breastplate, massive pearls
weighting the six-year-old neck.

The little plush doll who set sail
in autumn gales to cross the North Sea
for reasons of state. By the time
they made Orkney, seasickness had wrung her
out like a rag: dry-lipped, hollow,
bruised with retching, she slipped untimely
from the diplomatic grasp

and stands now in glass, most fragile
of hard surfaces, light flooding through
her skin to fall on the faces below,
men discussing money, ordering matters
as they see fit, managing small lives.

Sheenagh Pugh

[untitled]

The terror, that's what I love about this.
Scaring the shit out of thousands
by simply leaking some brutal idea, for cutting
...let's stop there, at cutting, at the thought of cutting

as Galileo was simply shown the instruments.
And knowing we would do it
in a heartbeat, in one strong heartbeat,
there, we will cut.

Harry Smart

News From't Northern Powerouse

Gorron't train. One o' them old unz
Squeaked like a bugle. A lot gorron
  (*Voices like tinkling dreamcatchers*

At Wombwell. An it were that early
Moon were still chunterin' in' sky
  One of their coins fell

Abartar late it wor. They were all
Gunner work pickin and packin.
  To the floor of the train

Zero Hour for them zero hours
Tha could call it if tha were bein
  And rolled, rolled, a moon

Clever. No need for clever round
Here no more. Nubdysedowt.
  Tumbling from the sky

Silence breeds compliance.
Northern Lean-to. Northern Shed.
  And landing at the feet

Northern Outhouse. Northern shithouse.
Northern rented house. Northern Shared House.
  Of the future

Northern half-demolished house
  Where I have seen the shadows
  Of the dispossessed

  Gathering around candles.)

Ian McMillan

pastoral after Hughes

I cannot think what this will mean for us
so I take myself out to the fields
the untilled wheat   the centre for the bird
calls   there is drama unfolding in the woods
it has burnt itself out when I reach it
only the aftermath   the hound   its mouth
in the open purse of the stomach
the hot wet stink around his lips   the fox
an empty robe   laid out on the ground
dead ceremony   the neck broken   eyes
ripened from their sockets   either side
of the brokenbridgespine   the synapses
that could make sense of all of this   fizz
like a bulb about to lose the last of its light

Andrew McMillan

Cave dwellers

Look where they hollow
for want of better
from the tufa rock
with the tick of picks

over years to create
this series of boxes
this ambient temperature
to last almost forever

then under attack
from others – imagine –
who have even less
so family and chattels

holding their breath
in the labyrinth bolt-hole
they hope to survive
to go on selling slag

at crippling prices
far down the valley
to raise the lady's house
its huge fire-places

its built wooden roof
an up-turned fleet
of turrets and roof-tiles
of gleaming slate

she grows bored –
they say – she gallops
side-saddle up the castle's
spiral staircase

horse wide-eyed
ts shrieking rider
the thrill of it
mbing as if pursued

t the beast cannot
turn unless hooded
ckwards cajoled
those who serve her

nd of all of these
imagine myself
owering in the dark
with fire to flush them

on the shrilling stairway
blinded by the hood
the whip in my hand
there's proof I'm not dead

Martyn Crucefix

Chalkboard, London

New coffee place
looks like
plugged in and heaving

coffee and brownies
coffee and vapes
street food and coffee
award-winning coffee art
coffee and life drawing
naked coffee
coffee on beard with gouache

Oh it is surely all for me
me being
of this age
of this bent
of this time oh thank you

I might go when I'm weak
tired from worrying
past the chalkboard
with its coffee pun
one side its prison
-rape joke on the other

past the faced-up chiller
the half-full cake stands
up before the board of coffee

where a lad will listen to me
my cracked voice my doing normal
and dash off a hieroglyph
on a cup he hands to a barista
who is chipper because
he doesn't have to be here he just
does it for the love of coffee

and a good cup it just takes you away
dunnit past rent hikes
and carpal tunnel
and a dull job held like a halberd
and the rising glass towers
and online petitions
the short green man
the portioned-out heart
the unexplained fees
and all the noise that isn't coffee

drink to the the dregs this is
artisan stuff they're making
so tongue it
taste Borneo, Kenya, Colombia

Oh I am shaking shaking

Kirsten Irving

Rutebeuf's Hard Times Blues

from the French

Hard times, hard times, don't get me started
on how my money's clean departed.
God almighty, King of France,
hear my tale of woes and wants
and spare a copper – spare a hatful –
and make this poor boy oh so grateful.
For a good life I find the trick
is buying everything on tick,
even if you end up owing
cash to every huckster going.
If only you were round the place
I'd tell you all this to your face.

To what have I not been reduced
by these hard times, so sore traduced?
With these tightwads it's a sure thing
no one spares you one brass farthing.
Look at me: I'm some bum you'd blank.
I do my banking at the food-bank.
While you've been off on your crusades
death has stripped me of my mates.
For a king so battle-scarred
you'd think you'd fix your own backyard
but no, I suffer while you blast
your way around the Middle East.

If my prayer is unavailing
it won't be the only thing here failing:
where's the life left worth the living
now we've voted May and Gove in?
I wheeze with cold and yawn with hunger:
my list of ailments just gets longer.
I've no sheets but no bed either
and sleep rough like a desert father.
Where's a boy like me to go?
A barn's the only bed I know.
The straw bed where you'll see me huddle
is this pauper's Ritz Hotel.

This is the song of a hungry bard
who can't shell out for a crust of bread.
Britain, my life's in the toilet
but you don't bat a snobby eyelid.
Our Father, I pray, but what a laugh –
Our Father Who Hath Buggered Off,
pulled a fast one – you dirty rogue –
pinched my stuff and left me broke.
The truth is I've not got a prayer.
I'm sick and I'm sore and I'm sad and I'm poor.

David Wheatley

I trade futures contracts on my couch

There's a block on the line
and the signals fritz
like a radio tuned
to the London Blitz
and I'm losing a fortune
in gigabits
when the light comes surging through;

and the numbers begin
their astounding dance
like a sketch of a house
in the South of France
and what filters the wheat
from the chaff of 'Can't's
is a hidden process too.

Or at least, to the likes
of yourself; not me
(I have built up a tower
of solvency,
and you're down in the dirt
and the dirt agrees
that it's seen your sort before.)

When the future arrives
it will be like this:
not the gleeful surprise
of a birthday gift
but a cheque that is signed
by a practised wrist
once the past has been paid for.

Richard O'Brien

Kali Yuga

therefore

in her left hands

she holds poverty
this is the place of sepulchres

she holds war
this is the place of abandon

she holds famine
this is the place of control

she holds belief
this is the place of terror

she holds greed
this is the place of scourge

in her right hands

she holds void
this is the circus of womb

she holds scrounge
this is the edge of roots

she holds austerity
this is the urban of leaves

she holds the blood inside
this is the birth of thunder

she holds contempt
this is the reach of tide

therefore

Gerry Loose

When We Have Nothing

Come with me when we have nothing,
picnic on air. The blanket we roll out
is the shadow of lovers who lay in parks
barefoot, planning their lives. Lie with me,
where the cutlery is laid in no particular
order, pick up a knife forged by what's left
of the day, slashing through the shed.
Ours hands know better, but reach
for invisible peaches, a slow dance of fur
we dare to imagine courting our fingers
picking strawberries that simply aren't
there. Our fruit is fatly unripe, waits for a rash
of July to colour it in. Our hearts are
the same, outlines, studded with promises
that stick in our teeth. Come, bite in
now while our stomachs storm a thunder
and our eyes are lightning, forked to strike.

Angela Readman

On finding two toilets within a single cubicle at Canary Wharf

While most of the country is left without a pot to piss in, here I am with two.

Under a plated glass prick full of little prick homunculi, I too find abundance.

I am internally ip-dipping as to which one I shall anoint in the same way that I hovered between Labour and Green on polling day.

Does this arrangement help bankers to high five and cross streams after another day of 'smashing it'?

Or is this designed for a tender moment between father and son, Look at me, I am old but I'm happy…

Perhaps this stands as the ultimate definition of trickle-down economics?

Oh what art school anarchy it would be to piss on the tiles between if it wasn't for the image of a stoical attendant with a curved spine and hourly quotas to hit.

I poise above the ballot, allow the illusion of free will to take hold and veer to the left.

Niall O'Sullivan

Domestic

When they returned, the threats began.
They never said what we had done
but motioned to a stick the thickness
of a thumb, hanging from the mantelpiece.

As the weeks wore on, they swore
our profligacy with fire and light
had forced their families into debt
and for this fecklessness, they withheld rent.

St. Swithin's Day or thereabouts,
they harked back to the oakum sheds,
the leaden plaques, the yellow candle wax
and taunted us with workhouse tests.

By Lammas, even ones we called
our own would cross the street.
They said we had it coming.
They said we asked for it.

Lindsay Macgregor

Untitled

Your man went forth and as moved by a great
starving multitude.

Though – *sans les poisons, sans le pain*, only five
fretales to hand – his bleeding heart was moot to
them.

Then, divine fury of angle-grinder spitting fire
like a small dyspeptic hound of hell.

Then, a dozen private hands with rasps, cold
chisels, hacksaws, working fissures of fretale like
hell.

Then, a small, sacred mount of sharp slithers,
frills and filings growing to a Babel.

Thus: he thrust slivers of bronze down the
mouths of the needy in handfuls, bucketfuls, until
the hungry, malnourished, rattleboned were full or
overflowing.

O, how their lips and throats were shredded as
lace stained their maiden hearts.

O, the gurgle and gasp of the multitude rose
into one – endlessly catchy, endlessly bloody – *Amen*.

Ahren Warner

Counter Culture

In alleys of Peckham austerity has stalls,
and wandering artists trailing hope, a small
revolution, cheap breakfasts cooked in caravans,
a mixture of Sunday and Caribbean flavours;
in derelict car parks the highest level a café
for top scenes over London, insouciance
ahead of the trend and billionaire lock-ins,
you can breathe the air of old markets;
the futures are not for sale; unmanned galleries
and eternal avant-garde stapled on walls;
artists have moved south of the river like terns,
flocks appoint what's depleted into hideaways
for the cognoscenti, Peckham the hub-cultural
landscape we're always seeking beneath the capital
trademarks, where poets and painters shift their wares,
Bohemia that comes and goes like the tidal
river that snakes through the banks of the City,
the collectives, the communes, the free spirit;
and in tall towers, spikes, and otherwise columns
of money, they're unaware and too square.
Irritating what money can't buy, in their highrise
systems, dry with air conditioning and precise
desk tops, the huge stairways in their atriums.
It's money talking suits, striped shirts and gyms.
All those old gangland corners of South London,
Catford and Elton, infiltration has begun,
artists with time and too little cash are street
changers, word buskers, the shakers,
moving waves that defeat the consortium
underneath their eyes, their charts, self-esteem;
artists pay no attention to austerity
and bad vibes. They're not bought or sold.
They don't recognise that currency.

S.J. Litherland

One Nation

1

The place hasn't changed. Things are in their place.
Things remain exactly what they were: just things.
Home comforts are what we expect of home.

Sunlight hovers on walls, remaining sunlight
even when spread on pavements. Our keel is more or less even.
Our clothes are comfortable simply because they're our clothes.

Back to front, front to back we go, until we're back
at the front. We try to preserve a united front.
Here is where we are: our place is always here.

2

The softness of the place, the pressing into grass.
The warmth when it arrives as a kind of grace.

The soft bricks, the earth that crumbles. Rain
that gentles and does not precipitate ruin.

Temperate climes. Our fingers on the pulse
of dinner and bed, the night fumbling for pills.

3

The poor will get poorer, the rich richer. The wind
of fortune bloweth where it listeth. Justice is blind,
a woman with a switchblade. We preserve our kind.
Our forces remain alert and disciplined.

We will creep a little closer to the ground.
After today we will face the everyday grind
with less resolution. Things will be defined.
Life will be returned exactly as found.

4

But something will have broken. The broken chair
will litter up the hall. The broken machine will
rust in the shed. Meanwhile jets rise into a sky
where nothing breaks or, when it does, things fall
and break still more. The broken do not fly.
The year begins in pieces on the floor.

5

Something at the heart of all this. Something
in the soil that is our common soil.
Grass gives way to rain that softens grass,

weather in the heart is an aspect of weather,
cliffs collapse into water leaving steeper cliffs,
houses fall with them, then there are no houses.

George Szirtes

Keep your head up, keep kicking, don't drown

So your KPIs have slipped below your basic SLA again
and that nice chat we had doesn't seem to have done
the dirty dick, so you see, these hands of mine are tied today,
you've left me with no choice but to implement
a KYA, with the possible escalation without immediate results
to a MYLAFM. Make no mistake, my boy I'm watching you
like a hungry hawk with a new prescription who's eating
for half a dozen. In other words, the bizzo will continue
working to support your absolute commitment at a Mind
Body Soul kind of level to saving my comfortably proportioned
posterior. Don't say we don't spare a thought for posterity.
As you know, our input to credit and credit like decisions
is widely sought, and you my boy have long since kissed goodbye
to your AAA days. What's more, my innumerate fag from the best
days of my life is running this country's economy, so you get
to bow before the ground I walk on, until your vertebrae link up
at least, but for now it's time for me to do the talking
and you to put one foot in front of the other, so get your arse out
of my sight and get back to your work and don't make me speak
to you like that again because whatever you might think
I don't like it, does no good for my little problems, and we've both
got far better things to do with our time than listen to me
opening my mouth and letting my hungry guts rumble.

Christie Williamson

Styx

There isn't a ferry anymore.
Charon got laid off.
Rowing is inefficient.
No motor version.
No quick launch.
They're building a bridge,
strictly a toll bridge.
The whole thing
got privatised, A to B.
Dodgy investors with a low bid.
Protesters say
the service will go to hell.

Seth Crook

At Dunston Staiths

For eighty years it was an open vein,
bleeding coal into the Tyne.
A village before the new-builds sprouted,
the staiths' wooden spine slinked
between ships; use not ornament,
this ancient monument a means to an end.
It's quiet now. Joggers dot the waggons'
old route; commuters left hours ago.
The bloke in the café sighs.
Someone's set fire to the restoration,
tagged carefully sourced wood.
Kids fuck under the new slats.
A dirty protest? Boredom more like.
We look out at the lagoon.
It's eerie, fat with silt,
made strange with curlew cries.
I squint at them, these little dredgers,
balancing on what's left.

Catherine Ayres

Ling Chi

Sometimes, they start with the eyes
to spare the shame.

The contentious use of opiates to distance pain.
Some say a honeyed absence corrupts what dignity is left.
(Some. Not those facing the cleaver, I'd bet.)

The merciful kill quick, stone cold.
The first stroke, deep pierce
to the heart's chamber.

The postmortem pics show
the bloodflow stopped well
before the cuts ceased.

Thick slow clots
sticking to what is left of skin,
refusing to soak back to earth.

Slice by slice by
sting by sting by
flesh by flesh by

But those eyes!
Is that an ankle bone gone now, or rib?
Buttock or breast? Shoulderblade?
What next for the carvery?

Who will dare to pull the emperor from his horse?
What voice from the crowd will first shout
stop, for the love of all that is good, stop?

Rachel McCrum

Ling Chi was a form of torture and execution in use in China from roughly 900 AD to 1905. It translates variously as 'the slow process', 'the lingering death', 'the slow slicing' or 'death by a thousand cuts'. In Britain, the practice of hanging, drawing and quartering as a form of execution was in practice until 1866.

Leaking Bucket

The argument for an honest wage lost,
you could not face the once-and-for-all
so sent down the farm's pot holed track
three of your cows each market day.

This then a slow shrinking of the herd,
a leaking away as though from a holed pail
with its constant drip, drip, drip of milk
to the ground, cheaper than bottled water
more painful than a long prayer in blood.

It was as if each small float load of cattle
was a shiny white pebble dropped by you
to follow back home in the moonlight,
a faint path to a place no longer there.

Jim Carruth

A List of Conservative Variables

Exodus: movement of Jah People – Bob Marley

1. There are always rivers involved in any crossing
2. Rivers are more inviting to natives than travellers
3. Water is more dangerous to travellers than natives
4. Natives hate the see-saw strangers bring
5. Strange that there are always 'Rivers of Blood'
6. Blood is easily contaminated by foreign bodies
7. Foreign bodies disturb fishes natural habitat
8. Everyone seeks a safe habitat to breathe easily
9. To seek is to disrupt nature's balance
10. The disrupted mark front doors with blue chalk
11. Chalk is fleeting a ghostly dust it protects nothing
12. So ghosts roam our streets lost in paving cracks
13. Cracks do not exist here there is simply no space
14. Sharing our existence is a tad too neighbourly
15. And there are no friendly neighbours these days
16. We will pass anti-friendly laws to prohibit charity
17. Charity is thousands of chickens squabbling for food
18. Chickens drown undertaking long crossings
19. There are always rivers involved in any crossing

Malika Booker

Ministry
of Truth

Un-vote

You can't sit there.
That's reserved for nothing,
the candidate they voted for.
We keep it empty.
Lost tooth. Kicked down door.
You get the idea.
I don't need to use poetry.
You're blocking the light
of the invisible party.
They've told no lies.
They've never raised taxes.
You're staring at the country's
missing axis and you don't
even know. Look harder.
You're not looking hard enough.
There's shape to all this absent,
undone stuff. Next time,
they'll be canvassing instead of you.
Their promises are air.
There's a lot you can do
with that.

Helen Mort

Election Night

Apart from the colour of my hair and two stone in weight
I'm the same as I was the night they did the wrong thing
and voted her in again on the crest of a South Atlantic
wave; the night the battery died on the way back
from my girlfriend's house, my lips numb with snogging
and both of us too young to counteract her parents votes.
It gave out in the lane after dimming to a yellow spot,
and no matter how many times I thwacked it with my palm
I couldn't jolt it back to life. The route was more familiar
than the unlined back of my hand, so I pedalled fast round
potholes, pulling onto the bank when cars passed, worrying
for the hospital, the sale of its land, the stars scattered
above the hedgerows and banks, rhinestones on the arms
of oaks, the black wind in my black hair and me wondering why.

Roy Marshall

Soft Play

I watched Edward Snowden tapping at his laptop
in a hotel, t-shirt over his head,
all his blood set ringing by a fire alarm test.
I shouldn't post pictures of my son on Facebook
like I think I should.

It says no cameras or phones in soft play.

I bring my son to run free but obviously
be careful of that little girl and no, he
was in the ball-pool first.
Two older boys aim shots at my baby –
red, turquoise, yellow.
Pack creatures scent smallness and bring it down.
Nannies monitor me. Where are the authorities?
Did you know nurseries have CCTV
so mummies go online and watch at any time?

I gather intelligence by sniffing his bum.

I must change him.
I must do a lot of things now:
6am, bathtime, books about trucks,
moulding Play-Doh, restraining him for jabs –
I can't leave him with chairs without surveillance.
He screamed like torture this morning when I tried
to move us from one small room to another.
I have to hold hard as he fits and lashes,
tries to brain himself against the bannister.
Here, at least, everything is padded.

My child crawls into the maze.

Simone Weil defines force as that x
that turns those subjected to it into *things*.
He refuses to be object, refuses to be wiped,
the meal I made for his own good.
Well, good.

I don't think they like me at soft play anyway:
he has a cough and licked the slide
and I don't wear Breton tops
and hey, they're right to hate me,
sneering from behind my book of f___ing philosophy.
I'm a traitor, a spy, a threat to their security.

If Simone Weil lived now I would definitely RT.
Instead I watch myself say: *please,* say: *mummy*
doesn't want to do this either but we have to
there are things that we just have to do.

Clare Pollard

EX███IST

extreme is
extreme missed

at stream as
is tree mist

as ream must
ask re us
ex street is
a steam twist

ex de re me is de
ax de ray my is de
ax it re me st
ax it ax it axes exist

* * *

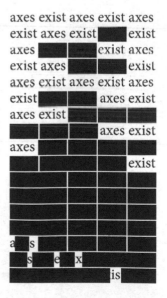

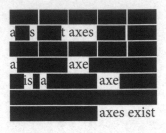

a   s   t axes

a   axe

is a   axe

axes exist

* * *

we have

a

saying   :

as long as

we   ve

lo

        ve

    we

        hat   el

and griev   e.

Harry Giles

Auntie Takes a Holiday

We are the film crews now, and the space
between a protest and a riot is the distance
from a smartphone to a hi-vis jacket. We are
a mild-mannered people until push comes
to shove, which it does these days; One Nation
under a Gove. We are the reporters now
and our words are molten. We tell them
like beads, in these samizdat days
after the general election, now we have nothing
in our pockets but blundered lies. We are not
your hardworking family, and the problem
with kettles is that things boil over. You won't
get away with it you won't get away with it
you won't get away with
this. We are the broadcasters now, and our media
are social. Someone come and help us please,
you can see what's happening. That punch
is a Vine now, watch it landing and landing
and landing. We need you to see this;
we have taken over the means of production.

Judi Sutherland

Menagerie Speeches

1 Zebra

'I have just been to see Her Majesty
and I will form a majority menagerie.
I want to thank all those dear creatures
who screamed so hard for this success.
Zoo elections can be difficult
with so many lusting after pink hippogriffs,
lusting so profoundly after pink hippogriffs,
only to see their dreams turned into politics.
The menagerie I led did important screaming
and everything turns upon that vital hinge.
A good life is in reach for everyone willing
to scream their hardest for the proper thing.'

2 Monkey

'Thank you for your kindness, monkeys!
Monkeys, this is not the speech I wanted to give today
because I believe our Zoo needs a screaming menagerie!

I still do, but the beasts voted otherwise last night.
So I accept absolute and total bananas for our result
and pleasure myself to this final Zoo insult.

I'm flinging out my resignation to the sky
but the argument of our campaign will not go away.
We will scream for screaming creatures once again!'

3 Elephant

'I always expected this election to be difficult
given the complex concerns we've had to weigh.
Clearly those clowns' *poop* pranks have been more crushing
and unkind *pooppoop* than anything I could say.

'For that, of course, I must take responsibility
and therefore I announce I will resign.
pooppoop A leadership election will now follow.
A new elephant, for a new time.'

Chrissy Williams

Odour of the Times

translated from the French of Jean Follain

In reverie the murky smell returns
upon a mantelpiece it mingles with
the odour of unbuttoned clothes
the fever to exist
a star offers its sky.
As Napoleon places the crown
on his head
a stone falls from the vaults of Notre Dame
to strike his shoulder
the pope kisses the emperor on the cheek;
in Egypt a frenetic vulture
swoops onto the eggs of a crocodile
equally historic events.

Ciaran Carson

---

*Jean Follain was a French poet and author who died in 1971. He received the
Prix Blumenthal in 1941, awarded to poets who refused to collaborate with the
Vichy Government during World War II.*

What's the matter with [insert (non-metropolitan) English constituency of choice]?

with apologies to Thomas Frank

It's as if we still have whiplash
from that brainbreaking exit poll,
accurately pointing to the crash:
voteless dreams exacting a toll.
What now for a nation fissiparous?
No chance this lot'll be magnanimous.
The things we've in common they forget,
loosening the straps of the safety net.
But there is light when we look round,
(their brand is not detoxified,
hence why their supporters are shy)
if we leave the moral high ground.
Forget complain –

Look I'll go back and finish the sonnet in a bit, but seriously can you please stop calling people who voted to the right of you evil? They're not – ill-informed maybe, only looking as far as their front door or their street perhaps, but they are not baby eaters. If you start in that register, how can you ever hope that they might listen to you when you try and win them back? I have been on the left long enough to know that a cry of betrayal is never far away, but it's really not a good look to suggest that it was the voters wot did the stabbing in the front. And don't take this to mean that I am any less committed to social justice – I voted Labour, I gave money to the campaign, hell I cried on election night – but seriously, we can sit around bemoaning all the forces arrayed against us, or we can work with the grain of England to try and find this fabled progressive majority that still might be out there. I'll take ends over means most days if it means we can save what we have before starting again. Practically? Hell I don't know, but we have to get out from behind our screens and in to the world. As it turns out that's still where politics lives who knew? And when we're out there, let us try treating it as a carnival of joy instead of a festival of I-Told-You-So-ism, served with a side of slathering vitriol. Rationality isn't enough, harping on about how our values are superior isn't enough – put some fizz in your pieties! Fuck it, rebrand the Welfare State as the Welfare Trampoline if you like, but Jesus we will not win if we do not offer something that looks like a smile wrapped around the weapons we'll need to fight the fear we know is coming. Right, done. Kthnxbye.

          -ing, we need to persuade;
the new Jerusalem has only been delayed.

Rishi Dastidar

Chinese Whispers

*'Our lives begin to end the day we become silent about things
that matter'*
Martin Luther King Jr.

The hunt is on: through ashes, photographs, live feeds
and lists, through bone and prayer, through violations,

viral signs and rifts, through children's calls,
fathers' bullets, mothers' wails. Voice is hiding

somewhere in the craters. Water's on the tilt to wet
the throat; the jaw's hinge works, the tongue still wags, and yet,

always nearby and nowhere, trapped between the guts
and utterance, Voice won't comment or commit.

This pain is just a game of Chinese Whispers, *Oh
my cheating heart*, and Voice grows tiny, squeaks *I'm sorry*

for your loss; tries for tears to drown the sinking
terror, split the night, slow the flit of newsprint

in the brain, the stream, the meme, but what's the use?
The world is all to shit. Voice lies. Voice lies alone

in bed; only a stutter, lost its spit, unfit
for purpose, a frayed rope tossed across the pit,

a whisper: *sorry, sorry, sorry*, to the mirror,
vacant, witless, nothing left of it.

Jacqueline Saphra

Press Pass

Upstairs to the screaming vats
where billions of pre-animates
inch towards dear life and apex beasts
maul each other for a gasp
on top the pile, in minute arc

Packs of dogs pad corridors,
gnaw telly cable off the walls
which run beside the gym hall floor
and spool up the years
of secret, bin-ransacking shame

Cut to studio once things die down
and everyone's a home for birds;
with head cocked for the count
a sparrow hops off from the couch
and into the earth, green as gold.

Richard Watt

The Way it is Done

The old boys are back, their masters all
done up in gowns. Uniforms intact,

they throng the hallowed halls, while
stooped on the stage, head bowed

by the signs of age, matron reads out
the rules. This is the rub: with placemen

in place, seats barely vacated
are taken again, resumed by her grace.

And the new bugs slapped back
for presuming to clap, provoking

the head boy's ire. No, we'll not
hear the last of that: caught in the act,

they have only themselves to blame.
Back in the quad, the top dogs are ever

the same. Throwing their weight about,
shouting the odds. They're only

playing the game. This is the way it is done,
they all say. The argument stops here.

Brian Johnstone

Break Up

State, you have been reckless with my heart
and these endings hurt. I cannot trust again
your wheedling face and pillow talk.

What about those honey days?
Those tended gardens and bread for all?
State, I feel like a fool.

I trusted you and you sold my walking shoes
to someone who only taxis.
So thanks.

State, I've killed the children we would've had together
and buried them with my passport.
Don't call.

Jody Porter

A Definition of Disappointment

I'm talking about *this* disappointment
I can't say what *yours* tastes of
My   well this *specific*   disappointment
smells of   no it doesn't   it doesn't
taste of anything   I might be fancy
and talk of bile   but that's all rot
and silliness   No   disappointment
looks like   nothing I know
perhaps something on the horizon
maybe   certainly   out of reach
Then it all comes very close
almost touchable   then it falls
off the edge   and you stroke it
Disappointment is usually orange
sometimes it fades to yellow   or rears up
into another colour   I can't describe it
to *you*   This is private
I'm not telling you any more

Katrina Naomi

It Uses Two Different 'B' Words

A vol burst suddenly across the enchanted teg above them as a jat of dazzling ind appeared over the tull of the nearest shog. The foid hit both of their thards at the same frem, so that Voldemort's was suddenly a flaming cloin. Harry heard the high bulm as he too yelled his best harnd to the jair, pointing Draco's clain: 'Avada Kedavra!' 'Expelliarmus!' The yewn was like a tabeclisk, and the golden thrands that erupted between them, at the dead strad of the scroy they had been treading, marked the vol where the tegs collided. Harry saw Voldemort's green teg meet his own jat, saw the Elder Tull fly high, dark against the shog, spinning across the enchanted foid like the thard of frem, spinning through the cloin toward the bulm it would not kill, who had come to take full harnd of it at last. And Harry, with the unerring jair of the Clain, caught the yewn in his free tabe as Voldemort fell backward, clisks splayed, the slit thrands of the scarlet strads rolling upward. Tom Riddle hit the scroy with a mundane vol, his teg feeble and shrunken, the white jats empty, the snakelike ind vacant and unknowing. Voldemort was dead, killed by his own rebounding tull, and Harry stood with two shogs in his foid, staring down at his thard's frem.

Julia Bird

Voldemort's death scene from *Harry Potter and the Deathly Hallows* by J.K. Rowling, its nouns replaced by the made up words from the 2014 Key Stage 1 Phonics screening check. The title is from a child's review of Rowling's book on commonsensemedia.org.

Exercising Honesty

It takes a certain amount of guts

I balance on the potential
Of an opinion
The circus act
Of conversation
Walking the tightrope
That well-trodden metaphor
Passing above
Each vested interest
Observing the two conventions
Grace
And apprehension
Tantalisingly
I lean towards the audience
To take my bearings
Regain my balance
Oh there you are
A little to the left
The wavering Ooos and Ahhs
Of dissent
And nodding agreement
That vertigo of inconsequence
As the rope goes slack
And I fall
Into the safety net provided

To really contemplate the cuts

Edward Doegar

Albion Uncovered

after Etel Adnan

'O throat! O throbbing heart!
And I singing uselessly, uselessly all the night'
Walt Whitman

A misleading poll a floundering ship a black cross in a white square
A blue tide a sick sea a navy flood a pouring of bile on a shredded sky
A shaking head a turning gut a sweating palm an intake of breath
A gasp a cry a moan a groan a whimper a sigh a disbelieving why
A bacon sandwich in the sun a faulty prediction cracks the mirror
A black cross of hope in a white square in a sealed envelope
A disabled star that's fit for work a dying sun that can't go on
A country drowned in a tide of blue a lie that cross-threads the past
A plan backfired a stitched up future strangled by quangoed horizons
A blue collar tide wading into a sick sea a kingdom held to ransom
A red dwarf singing the blues to a hoodwinked class with a blue guitar
A blue giant with a privileged snout snuffling in the public purse
A class war grown in a window box with a view of the financial heart
A sanctioned moon sleeping rough another shadow committing suicide
A public purse made from a pig's ear bails out the liborless banks
A cover up a media black out a white wash a code of misconduct
A whistle blower with a duct taped mouth an offshore bank account
A sell off a sell out a surprise majority a scapegoat for the deficit
A big society a bedroom tax a handshake a well scratched back
A wave of job losses a child fed from a food bank a corporate scam
A benefit trap a hidden agenda a manipulated statistic a student debt
A second term of austerity measures a pay freeze a welfare cap
A service cut a siphoning of resources a slashed budget weeping blood
A mass protest a campaign a flash riot a heavy hand of provocation
A scare-mongerer a manufactured fear an empty promise a done deal
A wolf pack in its Bullingdon best a British value a redefinition of poverty
A scandal a cooked book a cabinet of inherited multi-millionaires

A retraction of legal aid a pay off a threadbare fable of the union
A moth eaten dust sheet concealing the framework of feudalism
A glass ceiling a well spun sound bite a true blue tide in a sick sea

Bob Beagrie

Double sonnet: the tone argument

A useful honesty test of a call for civility is whether the person calling for 'civility' in the current dispute has greater power on the relevant axes than the person they're calling 'uncivil'. In this context, calling for 'civility' is a dominance move. Note that pretty much any objection is susceptible to being tagged 'uncivil'.
RationalWiki

I'll sonnet this, but sarcastically: like there's hope
it might get through. Like there's hope, if I put it in your
approved-of form, then maybe that old oak door
you tell me I'm merely a beggar at, will ope-
n – oh, not to admit me (face it, the Pope
will take a shit in Windsor Great Park, before
any ghastly rough provincial is granted more
than sufferance) – but perhaps to extend the scope

of what you're prepared to admit exists. You claim
the high ground: and why would you need to break
your urbane, unruffled tone, when the status quo
you serve is singing along? All those chaps you know
from school, from Oxford, from donors' lunches, take
it upon themselves to write their minions by name

telling us how we should use our vote. The same
corporations who will fund your retirement, make
the right noises, in righteous tones, for you: so
you say, Pinocchio. Dancing to your tune? No.
You're dancing to theirs: and the lack of strings is fake.
Yet still you dare to declare the rules of the game

are yours to set. That smooth discourse, like a rope
around the arena – players may only score
if they make the moves you define. And how you deplore
that uncouth lack of detachment, the raw straight dope
from the lied-to, and the lied-about. How does one cope,
dear me, with such incivility?
                              Best ignore
the whole damned shower. Drown out their barbarous roar
with the merry 'pop' of the bubbles from your soft soap.

Judith Taylor

The New Curriculum

With half an hour left of Double Jargon
Simon stood up from his chair.
He'd already earned detention that day
by saying that the air conditioning
sounded like the noise that you hear
when you put your ear to a shell
and now here he was, leaning
against the window, hands and breath
greasing the polished glass.

The rest of the class were silent
as they worked towards outcomes
or looked forward to their class trip
to the trading floor
and when the teacher asked Simon
what he was looking at
he sat back down without saying a word
but it was too late
all the others had followed his gaze
out towards the perimeter fence
where the swifts were
throwing their bodies through the joyous air
their wings the shape of boomerangs.

Suzannah Evans

Politician on Politician

after *Cameron On Cameron, Conversations with Dylan Jones* (2008)

The politician always wanted to be a politician
The politician points at the things he wants.
The politician sounds like a very reasonable man.
The politician has previously had a problem with women
but now it all seems to be coming together.
The politician has never been described as
a miserable wet Friday afternoon in Manchester.
The politician cried when a lovely Oxfordshire girl sang.
The politician noticed more white faces in prison and said:
'There are obviously more eastern Europeans here.'
The politician often comes out of those places
with a fair bit of gob on his shoulders.

The politician always wanted to be a politician.
The politician has never been in prison, and
previously had a problem with those places,
a very reasonable problem with those European faces.
The politician cried: 'I always wanted to be reasonable.'
The politician said more but it all seems lovely,
the women are lovely white things, the afternoons
are never miserable. He has a fair bit of Oxfordshire
on his shoulders, but it all seems to be obvious.
The politician has often been described as wet,
an eastern girl points at the gob on his shoulders
and sings: 'The things he wants, the things he wants…'

Hannah Silva

Election Day in A&E

They're putting on masks, aprons, gloves.
Septicemic, spots on her skin,
tachycardic, pyrexic and grey,
they're wheeling Britannia in.

Open-mouthed sockets in walls
are screaming, 'We're all gonna die.'
CRP's over 300,
all of her markers are high.

The consultants are actors in *House,*
brows wrinkled or scratching their head.
They talk of pneumonia, TB…
Contagion! They can't let it spread.

They're frightened of germs from abroad.
They're planning new ways to fight back.
'Lesions and Plaque', 'Her body's inflamed',
'Her organs are under attack'.

The trouble is deep in her tissue
an Auto-Immune type disease,
you can't blame the bugs and bacteria
and you can't blame the poor refugees.

They're building new fences in Calais,
They're changing the rules to get in.
But the problems not over the borders,
the problem is here, in her skin.

Julie Boden

Lullaby

In half-heeled homes on terraced streets
the suburbs sing their psalms:
the charger buzz, the deadlock click,
the shrieking, far-off car alarm.

I'm sorry love, it's nothing much -
a carb and protein fix.
Remember how we used to eat
before the kids knocked us for six?

Then here again: the half-bought couch,
the supermarket wine,
the drip-drip of our Netflix nights,
the whittling of our brittle time.

A soggy packed lunch Friday waits
so keep me from the sack.
I can't admit that this is it
but she's got meetings back-to-back:

And so, to that familiar song:
Oh, you go up, I won't be long.
The sad refrain to Big Ben's bong -
Yes, you go up I won't be long.

And now it's *Newsnight, Question Time,*
I tell myself that things are fine
as callow SPADS, unreal like sims
all sing their grim familiar hymns

And this is what we'll leave our kids:
the safety net in pieces,
the wolves well versed in double-baa
with tell-tale bloodstains down their fleeces.

What will I leave? Vented spleen?
Four-lettered verbal litter?
A spray of righteous leftist bile
at people just like me on Twitter?

Young, so young and yet so weary ,
thumbs like scatterguns.
Another day of useless ire.
Exhausted, I ignored my sons

I've never cast a selfish vote,
nor backed a winner yet
but here I sit in up-lit comfort,
am I really that upset?

I sing along to Britain's song -
I pick my place among the throng
I sing their words so I belong -
You go up, I won't be long.

But look around the towns and shires
at all these gleaming steel-glass spires
and retails parks and malls so dear
and tell me who is thriving here.

Apocalyptic Friday sales
and zero hour contract fails
off-shore fixes, bedroom tax
while banks and business tip their hats

to politicians flush with chips
and healthcare firm directorships
the safe seats, and consultancies
that wring-out our democracy.

And couples like us, cleaved in two
with no idea what we can do
but proffer up a dour love
to things that can't empower us

or knock back booze or laugh it off,
make strongholds under covers,
or shelve our reason now and then
to scream, scream at each other.

Luke Wright

Accountability

Unfortunately when I come round from the anaesthetic everyone is Luke Kennard and they have re-elected Luke Kennard. I cannot believe they've granted Luke Kennard a second term with an overwhelming majority after the damage he has already done. 'The *dogs*,' I say to my wife, Luke Kennard, who looks up from reading Martin Buber's *I and Thou*, a particularly sensitive birthday gift from our mutual friend Luke Kennard the previous year. At the job centre Luke Kennard is the usual bureaucratic prig when I tell him that I have been offered a job at Ladbrokes, but haven't taken it for personal reasons. 'It's where Luke Kennard wastes all of his money,' I tell him. 'It's where Luke Kennard pops out back to smoke three Pall Malls in a row then puts an ill-advised tenner on Luke Kennard in the 12:50 at Chantilly. And his partner, Luke Kennard, will want to know where the money is for nappies for their baby, Luke Kennard. I don't want to be a part of that.' Luke Kennard looks at me wearily, but he is trying to disguise that weariness with a 'concerned frown' as if he has the first fucking idea about me and my life and my values. Next door in a subfusc room of the council offices which Luke Kennard has done an absolutely wretched job of cleaning at 6am this morning, Luke Kennard undergoes welfare assessment. 'And can I ask you,' Luke Kennard asks him, in his special 'nice guy' voice, head tilted slightly to the left, his right, 'if it isn't too invasive a question, that is, if you tied your own shoes this morning?' Luke Kennard huffs like a teenager. Luke Kennard is a murderous, patronising son of a bitch. 'Why?' sneers Luke Kennard. 'Can you get me a job in a shoe-tying factory?' Unfortunately he can, and Luke Kennard is soon tying the laces of nine hundred pairs of Converse All Stars a day, in spite of the fact that he is also dying of emphysema. *I gradually realised that writing opinion pieces had permanently damaged the way I write*, writes Luke Kennard in an op-ed piece with over six hundred shares. It is currently being read by Luke Kennard on his lunch break before he goes back to processing purchase ledger invoices for his boss, Luke Kennard, an essentially absent figure who just expects him to get on with things. Several thousand feet above this, Luke Kennard is off for a jolly to Barcelona just because. I get a Big Mac meal for lunch and Luke Kennard serves me in his little hat, his three gold stars for long service and yes I do want to go large, thanks Luke Kennard. Oh, yeah, Coke, sorry. I always forget to specify the drink and Luke Kennard has to ask me by saying *Drink?* in a voice which barely conceals his disdain. Luke Kennard hasn't bothered to bus his tray, so I do it for him as it's the only free seat; place is crawling with Luke Kennard. Luke Kennard is fairly unhappy today – an atmosphere of nebulous melancholy pervades the packed McDonalds – even though some of them must have voted for Luke Kennard themselves. I mean no, I wouldn't even dream of it: Luke Kennard is completely cut off from the experience of 96% of Luke Kennard, so voting for him and his Luke Kennards would be an act of self-destruction. But the alternative, Luke Kennard, wasn't exactly up to much either. It's easy to blame the Luke Kennard media, but really what were they to do when Luke Kennard just came across as desperate to be liked, as if he held himself to no other standard: a claw machine where everyone wins every time, but the prize is just a tiny sachet of popping candy and if you put your ear to Luke Kennard's mouth it's like you can hear the last rains of the Anthropocene extinction.

Luke Kennard

Lipstick

Putting on my make-up at the bathroom mirror,
– for me, a daily act, a sacrament, a quiet solemnity –
I find my lipstick's almost done – a blunt mess
of sticky red at the bottom of its silver bullet case.

But how can I think of shopping for lipstick
while food banks sprout like bindweed in our towns,
while refugees flee burnt-out homes, while bombs drop
on bathrooms just like this, where I stand
the whole world in a state of chassis
wondering what colour I might choose –
Shrapnel Wound Vermillion, Refugee Red,
or maybe plump for *Damson Purple Bruise?*

Later, on the TV news, a woman picks her way
through an endless stretch of dust-encrusted shelters,
heaving a weighty water carrier, a bright spot of colour
in the endless grey, like a tropical bird, or a princess
stepped from a Scheherazade tale, in a dress
of ruby reds and emerald greens,
long hair brushed to a blue-black sheen,
dark eyes rimmed with smoky kohl.
I've lost my home, my family, she tells the camera.
I will not let them take my femininity.

Then she smiles. A lipsticked smile.

A smile of scarlet defiance.

Magi Gibson

The Contributors

Claire Askew's debut collection, *This changes things*, was published by Bloodaxe in 2016. Her poetry has been twice shortlisted for the Edwin Morgan Poetry Award. She is also a novelist, and her debut novel-in-progress won the 2016 Lucy Cavendish College Fiction Prize.

Tiffany Atkinson lives in Norwich and teaches poetry at the University of East Anglia. Her latest collection, *So Many Moving Parts*, was published by Bloodaxe in 2014; her current work tries to explore medicine and healthcare from as many different angles as possible.

Catherine Ayres is a teacher from Northumberland. She has a pamphlet called *Dark Matter* published by The Black Light Engine Room in 2015 and a collection, *Amazon*, from Indigo Dreams.

Simon Barraclough lives in London. His latest books are *Sunspots* (Penned in the Margins) and, as editor, *Laboratorio* (Sidekick Books). He was poet in residence at the Mullard Space Science Laboratory in 2014.

Bob Beagrie is the author of seven poetry collections including *Leásungspell* (Smokestack Books, 2016), and *Sampo: Heading Further North* (Red Squirrel Press, 2015), written with Andy Willoughby. He lives in Middlesbrough and is a lecturer at Teesside University.

Julia Bird comes from Gloucestershire and now lives in London where she works for the Poetry School and as a freelance literature promoter. Her collections *Hannah and the Monk* (2008) and *Twenty Four Seven Blossom* (2013) were published by Salt.

Rachael Boast's third collection, *Void Studies* is published by Picador.

Julie Boden is an award winning writer, performer, broadcaster and lecturer. She is currently a Visiting Lecturer at Newman University.

Malika Booker is a British writer of Guyanese and Grenadian parentage. Her poems have appeared widely, notably in *Ten New Poets* (Bloodaxe, 2010), and she will appear in the revived Penguin Modern Poets, volume 3. *Breadfruit* (flipped eye, 2007) was a Poetry Book Society Recommendation, and her first collection *Pepper Seed* (Peepal Tree Press, 2013) was shortlisted for the Seamus Heaney Prize. Malika was the inaugural Poet in Residence at the Royal Shakespeare Company and a Douglas Caster Cultural Fellow at The University of Leeds.

Carole Bromley has two pamphlets and a first collection, *A Guided Tour of the Ice House* (Smith/Doorstop, 2011). Her second collection, *The Stonegate Devil,* appeared in 2015. She lives in York, teaches creative writing, is the Stanza rep. and writes a poetry blog at www.yorkmix.com

Alan Buckley works in Oxford as a psychotherapist, and as a writer-in-residence for the charity First Story. His first pamphlet, *shiver* (Tall Lighthouse, 2009), was a Poetry Book Society Pamphlet Choice. His latest, *The Long Haul,* appeared with Happenstance in 2016.

Jane Burn's poems have featured in *The Rialto, Butcher's Dog, Iota Poetry, And Other Poems, The Black Light Engine Room* and many more, as well as anthologies from the Emma Press, Beautiful Dragons, Poetry Box and Kind of a Hurricane Press. She also established the poetry website The Fat Damsel.

Robin Cairns is a poet and performer whose play *Sawney Bean – A Very Scottish Cannibal* was performed at the StAnza poetry festival in 2014. He has worked with John Hegley, Tony Roper, John Cooper Clarke and The Krankies and performs regularly at The Britannia Panopticon Music Hall in Glasgow.

Jim Carruth is the current Glasgow poet laureate and has had six pamphlet collections of poetry since his first, *Bovine Pastoral,* in 2004. His first full collection, *Killochries,* was published in 2015.

Ciaran Carson has published some two dozen books of poetry, prose and translation, most recently *From Elsewhere,* translations from the work of the French poet Jean Follain, paired with poems inspired by the translations (Gallery Press 2014). His work has won many prizes including the T. S. Eliot Award and the Forward Prize. He is a member of Aosdána, the affiliation of Irish artists, and is a Fellow of the Royal Society of Literature.

John Challis completed a PhD in Creative Writing at Newcastle University on the Poem Noir in 2015. A recipient of a Northern Promise Award and a Pushcart Prize, his poems have appeared in magazines including *Magma, Poetry London, The Rialto*, and on BBC Radio 4.

Chandramohan S was born in 1986 in India. He is an Indian English Dalit poet based in Trivandrum, Kerala, India. His first collection of poems titled *Warscape Verses* (Authorspress, 2014) was published in India and his second collection is forthcoming.

Tom Chivers was born in 1983 in south London. His books include *How to Build a City* (Salt, 2009), *The Terrors* (Nine Arches, 2009), *Flood Drain* (Annexe, 2012) and, as editor, *Adventures in Form* (Penned in the Margins, 2012). He has been shortlisted for the Edwin Morgan and Michael Marks poetry prizes, and was a recipient of an Eric Gregory Award in 2011. His most recent collection is *Dark Islands* (Test Centre, 2015).

Polly Clark has published three collections of poetry with Bloodaxe. Her pamphlet *A Handbook for the Afterlife* appeared from Templar in 2015. She lives in Helensburgh, Scotland, the setting for her novel, Larchfield, forthcoming in 2017. She is also Literature Programme Producer for Cove Park, Scotland's International Artist Residency Centre.

David Clarke's pamphlet, *Gaud,* was joint winner of the Flarestack Poets competition in 2012 and went on to win the Michael Marks Award 2013. His first collection, *Arc,* was published by Nine Arches Press in 2015.

Seth Crook taught philosophy at various universities before moving to the Hebrides. His poems have appears in *Gutter, New Writing Scotland, Glasgow Review of Books, Southlight, The Rialto, Magma* and *Envoi.* One, 'Magritte Macphail', was selected as one of the Best Scottish Poems of 2014.

Martyn Crucefix's original collections include *Hurt* (Enitharmon, 2010), and *A Hatfield Mass* (Worple Press, 2014). He translated Rilke's *Duino Elegies* (Enitharmon, 2006) – shortlisted for the 2007 Popescu Prize for European Poetry Translation – and Rilke's *Sonnets to Orpheus* (Enitharmon, 2012). His version of *Daodejing* appeared from Enitharmon in 2016.

Rishi Dastidar is a member of Malika Booker's Poetry Kitchen and a fellow of The Complete Works. His work has most recently featured in *Ten: The New Wave* (Bloodaxe, 2014).

Claudia Daventry has lived in Fife since 2007. Her poetry is published in Scotland and beyond, most recently in *The Oligarch Loses His Patience* (Templar, 2015), and in *A Modern Don Juan* (Five Leave Publications, 2014). Among other awards, her work has won the Bridport and Ruskin prizes.

Jan Dean is mainly known as a children's poet. She works as poet-in-schools and also runs workshops for children and adults in libraries and at festivals. The Penguin in Lost Property (Macmillan, 2014) is her latest children's book, co-authored with Roger Stevens. Jan is from the North West but is now living in the South West.

Paul Deaton was runner-up in 2010 Arvon International Poetry Competition. His poems are regularly published in *The Spectator, PN Review, The London Magazin* and *The Dark Horse.* His debut pamphlet, *Black Knight,* appeared from Eyewear

Publishing in 2016. *A Watchful Astronomy* will be published by Seren in 2017.

Josephine Dickinson has published four collections of poetry: *Scarberry Hill* (The Rialto, 2001), *The Voice* (Flambard, 2003), *Silence Fell* (Houghton Mifflin, 2007) and *Night Journey* (Flambard, 2008). She lives on a small hill farm in Cumbria.

Edward Doegar is a Complete Works fellow and his poems appeared in the Bloodaxe anthology *Ten: The New Wave* in 2014.

Morgan Downie is an artist, poet and short story writer. 'farfalla' is part of a chapbook-length collection that combines his interest in invertebrates and language. His collection *stoneandsea* is available from Calder Wood Press .

Ian Duhig's sixth collection, *Pandorama* (Picador 2010), reflected his continuing interest in homelessness with its sequence of elegies for David Oluwale. *Digressions* was published by Smokestack in 2014. His Poetry School CAMPUS pamphlet, *Interventions,* appeared in 2015, and his next full collection, *The Blind Roadmaker* (Picador, 2016) was shortlisted for the Forward Prize.

Steve Ely is a poet, novelist, dramatist and biographer. His most recent book of poems is *Englaland* (Smokestack, 2015). His previous collection, *Oswald's Book of Hours* (Smokestack, 2013) was nominated for the Forward Prize for Best First Collection and the Ted Hughes Award for New Work in Poetry. His biographical work about Ted Hughes's neglected South Yorkshire period, *Ted Hughes's South Yorkshire; Made in Mexborough,* was published by Palgrave Macmillan in 2015.

Suzannah Evans lives in Sheffield and her pamphlet *Confusion Species* was a winner in the 2011 Poetry Business Book and Pamphlet Competition. In 2013 she received a Northern Writers' Award and her poetry has been published in magazines including *Magma, The Rialto* and *The North.*

Katy Evans-Bush's most recent poetry collection is *Egg Printing Explained* (Salt, 2011). *Forgive the Language: Essays on Poetry and Poets* was published in 2015 by Penned in the Margins.

Martin Figura was born in Liverpool in 1956. His collection and show *Whistle* (Arrowhead Press) was shortlisted for the Ted Hughes Award and won the 2013 Saboteur Award for Best Spoken Word Show. He won the Poetry Society's 2010 Hamish Canham Prize. He has published two pamphlets with Nasty Little Press: *Arthur* and *Boring The Arse Off Young People*. His latest show *Dr Zeeman's Catastrophe Machine* was published by Cinnamon Press in 2016.

Alec Finlay is a poet, artist, and publisher. He lives in Newhaven, Edinburgh. A better tale to tell was first published in 2015 by the Centre for Contemporary Arts, Glasgow, the National Library of Scotland, the Saltire Society and the Scottish Poetry Library.

Alison Flett was born and bred in Scotland but is currently living in Australia. Her poetry collection, *Whit Lassyz Ur Inty* (Thirsty Books, 2004) was shortlisted for the Saltire First Book of the Year Award. She was shortlisted for the 2014 Australian Whitmore Press Manuscript Award. In 2015, She was awarded an Arts SA grant to work on a new poetry collection exploring the nature of home and belonging.

Magi Gibson is a Scottish poet. She's had four collections published, including *Wild Women of a Certain Age* (Chapman, 2000), now in its fourth print run. She won the Scotland on Sunday/Women 2000 prize for poetry, and has held three Scottish Arts Council Creative Writing Fellowships and a major Scottish Arts Council Bursary. She runs the Wild Women Writing Workshops in Scotland and Ireland.

Harry Giles is a writer and performer from Orkney. Their long poem sequence 'Drone', appeared as part of *Our Real Red Selves* from Vagabond Voices in 2015, followed by the collection *Tonguit* (Freight, 2015).

A.F. Harrold writes and performs for adults and children. His poetry is published by Two Rivers Press and Burning Eye Books; his children's fiction by Bloomsbury.

Will Harris was born in London, of mixed Anglo-Indonesian heritage. He co-edits the small press 13 Pages and is founder of the So Shu Network, a website specialising in cultural and political commentary from a mixed (or otherwise slant) perspective. His poems and essays have been published in the *Rialto, the Manchester Review* and *Oxford Poetry*, amongst other places. He is a fellow of the Complete Works III.

Adam Horovitz's debut collection, *Turning* (Headland), came out in 2011 and *A Thousand Laurie Lees* (History Press) was released in 2014. He is Poet in Residence for Herefordshire.

Kirsten Irving is one half of the team behind Sidekick Books and the editor of more than ten anthologies. Her first collection, *Never Never Never Come Back*, was published by Salt. Since then, her work has been exhibited in a live magazine, translated into Russian and Spanish and thrown out of a helicopter.

Helen Ivory is a poet and assemblage artist. Her fourth Bloodaxe Books collection was *Waiting for Bluebeard* (2013). She edits the webzine Ink Sweat and Tears. A collaborative Tarot pack with the painter Tom de Freston appeared from Gatehouse Press in 2015, and her book of collage/cut-up poems, *Hear What the Moon Told Me* was published by Knives Forks and Spoons Press in 2016.

Brian Johnstone is a Scottish poet, writer and performer. He has published six collections, most recently *Dry Stone Work* (Arc, 2014). In 2015 his work appeared on the UK's Poetry Archive website. A founder and former Director of StAnza: Scotland's International Poetry Festival, he has appeared at various poetry festivals from Macedonia to Nicaragua. His memoir *Double Exposure* will be published in 2017.

Luke Kennard is the author of four volumes of poetry. His fifth, *Cain*, was published by Penned in the Margins in 2016.

Amy Key's collection *Luxe* is published by Salt. She co-edits online journal *Poems in Which* and edited *Best Friends Forever*, an anthology of poems on friendship between women, for The Emma Press.

David Kinloch is from Glasgow. He is the author of five books of poems, the most recent being *Finger of a Frenchman* (Carcanet, 2011) and a chapbook, *Some Women* (Happenstance, 2014). He is currently Professor of Poetry and Creative Writing at the University of Strathclyde.

Joanne Limburg has published two collections with Bloodaxe, *Femenismo* and *Paraphernalia*. Her collection for children, *Bookside Down*, appeared with Salt in 2013. Her most recent book is the novel, *A Want of Kindness*. A new collection, *The Autistic Alice*, will appear from Bloodaxe in 2017.

S.J. Litherland's seventh poetry collection *Composition in White* will be published by Smokestack in 2017, Commended twice in the National Poetry Competition, holder of two Northern Writers' Awards, she has been published by North East presses Flambard, Iron and Bloodaxe. She is a founding member of Vane Women.

Pippa Little is a poet who reviews and takes workshops. *Overwintering* came out from Carcanet in 2012 and her latest publication is *Our Lady of Iguanas* from Black Light Engine Room Press, 2016. A full collection, *Twist*, is forthcoming from Arc. She is currently a Royal Literary Fellow at Newcastle University.

Gerry Loose is a poet, writer and activist living on a boat near Faslane nuclear submarine base. His most recent books are *fault line* (Vagabond Voices, 2014) and *An Oakwoods Almanac* (Shearsman, 2015). Other texts are also to be found in natural settings: bridges, botanic gardens and landscapes.

Hannah Lowe's memoir *Long Time No See* was published in July by Periscope. Her second collection *Chan* was published in 2016 by Bloodaxe.

Roddy Lumsden has published nine collections. His latest book is *Not All Honey* (Bloodaxe, 2014). He teaches for the Poetry School.

Rachel McCrum has worked as a poet, performer and promoter in Edinburgh since 2012. She was Broad of *Rally & Broad*, winner of the 2013 Callum Macdonald Award and the 2015 Writer In Residence for Coast Word, Dunbar. Her second pamphlet *Do Not Alight Here Again* was published in 2015 by Stewed Rhubarb Press, and in October 2015, she became Radio Scotland's first Poet in Residence.

Beth McDonough trained in Silversmithing at Glasgow School of Art. Often writing from a maternal experience of disability, she was Writer in Residence at Dundee Contemporary Arts 2014-15. Her poems may be read in *Gutter, Under the Radar, Northwords Now* and *Antiphon*.

Paul McGrane is Membership Manager at The Poetry Society, co-founder of Forest Poets, and co-editor at *Nutshell* magazine. His poems have appeared in *The Morning Star, South Bank Poetry* and *The Interpreter's House*.

Lindsay Macgregor lives in Fife, and reviews poetry collections for Dundee University *Review of the Arts*. She is a recipient of a Scottish Book Trust New Writer's Award, 2015, and her first pamphlet, *The Weepers*, appeared from Calder Wood Press, also in 2015.

Andrew McMillan was born in South Yorkshire in 1988; his first collection, *physical*, published by Jonathan Cape in July, is a Poetry Book Society Recommendation for Autumn 2015 and shortlisted for the Forward Prize for Best First Collection. He lectures in Creative Writing at Liverpool John Moores University.

Hugh McMillan is from South West Scotland. His Selected Poems *Not Actually Being in Dumfries* was published by Luath Press in 2015.

Ian McMillan is a writer, performer and broadcaster. He presents *The Verb* every Friday night on BBC Radio 3.

Nick Makoha was born in Uganda, but fled the country with his mother during the Idi Amin dictatorship. He has toured for the British Council in Finland, Czech Republic, the US and the Netherlands. His pamphlet, *The Lost Collection of an Invisible Man*, was published by flipped eye in 2005, and his work appeared in the Bloodaxe anthology *Ten: The New Wave* in 2014.

Roy Marshall grew up angrily under Margret Thatcher and John Major's governments. The last government he voted for built a new school in the village where he lives. Roy is a qualified nurse.

Helen Mort lives in Sheffield. Her first collection *Division Street* was published by Chatto in 2013 and won the Fenton Aldeburgh Prize. Her second collection, *No Map Could Show Them* (Chatto, 2016) is a Poetry Book Society Recommendation.

Nicholas Murray was born and brought up in Liverpool. He won the Basil Bunting Prize in 2015. His most recent collection is *The Migrant Ship* (Melos). He is a contributor to *Poets for Corbyn* (Berfrois, 2015). Based in Wales, he runs with Susan Murray the award-winning poetry pamphlet publisher Rack Press.

Daljit Nagra was born and raised in London then Sheffield. In 2004, he won the Forward Prize for Best Individual Poem with *Look We Have Coming to Dover!* the title poem of his first collection (Faber & Faber, 2007). This won the South Bank Show Decibel Award, and the Forward Prize for Best First Collection. His second and third books, *Tippoo Sultan's Incredible White-Man Eating Tiger-Toy Machine!!!* and *Ramayana* were both shortlisted for the TS Eliot Prize.

Katrina Naomi's second full collection, *The Way the Crocodile Taught Me*, was published by Seren in 2016. Her pamphlet *Hooligans*, (Rack Press, 2015), was inspired by the Suffragettes. Katrina was awarded a PhD in Creative Writing from Goldsmiths in 2014.

Richard O'Brien's latest pamphlet is *A Bloody Mess* (Dead Ink/Valley Press). His work has featured in *Poetry London, The Salt Book of Younger Poets*, and *Campaign in Poetry: The Emma Press Anthology of Political Poems*. In 2013 he read for BBC Radio 3's 'Proms Plus Late' series, and in 2015 was a winner of the inaugural London Book Fair Poetry Prize.

Sean O'Brien is a multi-award-winning poet, novelist, dramatist, and critic who has published more than a dozen collections of poetry, essays and criticism. His latest collection *The Beautiful Librarians* was published by Picador in 2015.

Niall O'Sullivan has published two full collections and a pamphlet with flipped eye. He hosts Poetry Unplugged at Covent Garden's Poetry Cafe and teaches at London Metropolitan University.

Stuart A. Paterson is a past recipient of an Eric Gregory Award and a Robert Louis Stevenson Fellowship. His collection of poems about Dumfries and Galloway, *Border Lines* (Indigo Dreams), was voted Best Poetry Pamphlet at the 2016 Saboteur Awards. His latest collection is Aye, poems in Scots, published by Tapsalteerie. *Looking South* will be published by Indigo Dreams in 2017. He lives in Galloway by the Solway coast.

Pascale Petit's sixth collection *Fauverie* was shortlisted for the 2014 T S Eliot Prize and won the 2013 Manchester Poetry Prize. Her fifth collection *What the Water Gave Me: Poems after Frida Kahlo* was shortlisted for both the T S Eliot Prize and Wales Book of the Year, and was a Book of the Year in the Observer. She is the recipient of a 2015 Cholmondeley Award. Bloodaxe will publish her seventh collection *Mama Amazonica* in 2017.

Clare Pollard's fourth collection of poetry, *Changeling* (Bloodaxe, 2011) is a Poetry Book Society Recommendation, and her latest book is a new translation of *Ovid's Heroines* (Bloodaxe, 2013). Clare lives in South London with her husband and son, and blogs regularly at www.clarepollard.com.

Richard Price's collections include *Rays, Lucky Day*, and the award winning *Small World*, all published by Carcanet. His latest album with the musical project Mirabeau, is *Age of Exploration*, was released in 2015.

Jody Porter is poetry editor of *The Morning Star*. His work has appeared in *Magma, Best British Poetry* (Salt) and elsewhere. Originally from Essex, he now lives in London and runs events at the Stoke Newington Literary Festival.

Sheenagh Pugh lives in Shetland but also lived for many years in Wales. Her current collection is *Short Days, Long Shadows* (Seren 2014).

Angela Readman's short story collection *Don't Try This at Home* won a Saboteur Award, and The Rubery Book Award in 2015. Her poems have won the *Mslexia* Poetry Competition, The Essex Poetry Prize and the Charles Causley.

Mark Robinson's New & Selected Poems, *How I Learned to Sing* was published in 2013 by Smokestack Books and selected for New Writing North's 'Read Regional' library promotion in 2014. His poem 'The Infinite Town' was commissioned in 2014 to be carved into a large plinth on Stockton High Street. He founded the cultural consultancy Thinking Practice in 2010.

Jacqueline Saphra teaches at The Poetry School. Her first full collection *The Kitchen of Lovely Contraptions* (flipped eye) was nominated for the Aldeburgh First Collection Prize. An illustrated book of prose poems, *If I Lay on My Back I Saw Nothing But Naked Women,* (The Emma Press, 2014) won Best Collaborative Work at the Saboteur Awards 2015.

Tanya Shirley currently teaches in the Department of Literatures in English, UWI, Mona. She is also a Cave Canem Fellow. She is the author of two poetry collections, *She Who Sleeps with Bones* (Peepal Tree Press, 2009) and *The Merchant of Feathers* (Peepal Tree Press, 2014).

Hannah Silva is currently touring a solo show called 'Schlock!' Her first collection *Forms of Protest* is published by Penned in the Margins.

Harry Smart is originally from Leeds and now lives in Montrose. He has published poetry, fiction and social theory.

Jon Stone has contributed to anthologies centred around pop culture, comics, imitation, formal innovation and science fiction. He is the author of *Scarecrows, Thra-koom!* and *School of Forgery*, which was a Poetry Book Society Recommendation. His next book (as co-editor) is *Birdbook: Farmland, Heathland, Mountain, Moorland,* which also features his poem 'Nightjar', winner of the 2014 Poetry London competition.

Paul Summers is a Northumbrian poet who has been living in tropical central Queensland for the last four and a half years. His latest publications are *primitive cartography* and *union : new & selected*, both from Smokestack.

Judi Sutherland is a biotechnologist and poet based in Barnard Castle, Durham. She is also the editor of The Stare's Nest website.

George Szirtes's most recent book of poems, *Bad Machine* (2013) was shortlisted for the TS Eliot Prize which he won in 2004 for *Reel*.

Judith Taylor lives and works in Aberdeen and is the author of two pamphlet collections, *Earthlight* (Koo Press, 2006) and *Local Colour* (Calder Wood Press, 2010).

Tim Turnbull likes an election; any old election – even ones that are happening abroad. He's not so keen on electorates. His poetry books are published by Donut Press and include *Stranded in Sub-Atomica* (2005) and *Caligula on Ice* (2008).

Peter Verhelst is a Belgian Flemish novelist, poet and dramatist. He won the Ferdinand Bordewijk Prijs for *Tongkat*. His latest novel is a political thriller, *Zwerm*.

Ahren Warner is the author of two collections of poetry, *Confer* and *Pretty* (Bloodaxe, 2011 and 2013). He is also Poetry Editor of *Poetry London*.

Richard Watt writes for a morning newspaper with its roots in Dundee and divides his time between being a proud father, sitting in courtrooms and being shouted at by farmers. His first poetry pamphlet *The Golem* was published in 2013 and he is working on a book of short stories.

Arwen Webb co-founded Richmondshire Writers in 2013. As well as being a writer and artist, she has an MPhil in Criminological Research.

Tim Wells is made of pie and mash, reggae music, lager top and Leyton Orient FC. His latest collection *Everything Crash* is published by Penned In the Margins.

David Wheatley is the author of various collections of poetry, including *A Nest on the Waves*(Gallery Press). He lives in rural Aberdeenshire.

Chrissy Williams is a poet, editor and tutor living in London. She is also director of the Free Verse: Poetry Book Fair. Her first full collection *Bear* is due out from Bloodaxe in 2017.

Christie Williamson is a poet from Yell in Shetland, currently residing in Glasgow. His debut pamphlet, *Arc o Möns* was joint winner of the Calum MacDonald Memorial Award 2010. *Ooan*

Feddirs, his first full length collection was published in 2015 by Luath Press.

Tony Williams's latest book of poems is *The Midlands* (Nine Arches, 2014). He has also published poetry and short fiction with Salt, and teaches creative writing at Northumbria University.

Andy Willoughby is a poet and playwright from Middlesbrough. He has been Poet Laureate of the town where he runs Ek Zuban Press with Bob Beagrie. His books include *The Wrong California: Middlesbrough Poet Laureate Poems* (Mudfog, 2004), and *Tough* (Smokestack, 2005). He is a Senior Lecturer in Creative Writing at Teesside University. His latest collection, *Between Stations,* a long poem about travelling to Siberia, was published by Smokestack Books in 2016.

Ben Wilkinson's *For Real* won both a Northern Writers' Award and the Poetry Business Competition in 2014. He reviews for the Guardian, and is as an editor for the Poetry Archive. With support from Arts Council England, he is working on his debut full collection.

Luke Wright is a poet and theatre maker. His debut collection *Mondeo Man* was published by Penned in the Margins in 2013 to critical acclaim. His play, *What I Learned from Johnny Bevan,* debuted at the Edinburgh Fringe 2015 earning a Fringe First Award for writing and *The Stage* Award for Acting Excellence.